Ōtsu-e

Japanese Folk Paintings

from the Harriet and Edson Spencer Collection

Matthew Welch

The Minneapolis Institute of Arts

Contents

Preface

Japanese art objects of astonishing technical refinement and breathtaking opulence are renowned throughout the world. It is all the more humbling to discover, therefore, that even objects created by anonymous artists for use by common people are often disarmingly beautiful. Transcending the limitations of their modest materials, these unsung craftsmen produced works of great confidence and vitality, and even the poorest household possessed utilitarian objects of extraordinary artistic design.

It is to their credit that Harriet and Edson Spencer, during their time in Japan, looked beyond the acclaimed master artists of Japanese history and recognized the unassuming beauty of Ōtsu-e. Making use of the Japan Folk Crafts Museum established in 1936 by Yanagi Sōetsu, the Spencers educated themselves about this unique art form. Their collection of representative examples of Ōtsu-e, amassed over nearly thirty years, is one of the largest outside of Japan. This exhibition and catalogue are the result of their continued enthusiasm and generosity in sharing the works which have brought them so much pleasure over the years. I am honored to have been given the opportunity to study and write about this remarkable group of paintings.

The realization of this catalogue has depended upon the dedication and talents of many friends and colleagues. I would like to thank Robert Jacobsen, curator of Asian art, for his encouragement and unfailingly sound advice. I am deeply indebted to Tanji Chizuko for the many hours she patiently spent helping with translations and deciphering inscriptions written on Ōtsu-e. In the early stages of the project, Catherine Parker, curatorial assistant, provided invaluable technical support. I am grateful to Sarah Blick, Catherine's successor, for typing the manuscript and for offering many helpful suggestions. I would also like to acknowledge Elisabeth Sövik for her meticulous and sensitive editing; Ruth Dean for her great skill in designing this catalogue; and Gary Mortensen and Robert Fogt for their consistently outstanding photography. As always, the museum's registrars and exhibition technicians saw to the installation of the show with painstaking care and efficiency.

Matthew Welch
Assistant Curator of Asian Art

Collectors' Foreword

We first visited Japan in 1958. At that time we knew little, in fact almost nothing, of the richness and beauty of Japanese arts and crafts. In 1959, we returned to take up residence for five years in Tokyo, where Ed was Far East regional manager for Honeywell. During those years, Harriet began buying scroll paintings, woodblock prints, ceramic pieces, and antique furniture. With no real thought of building a collection, we bought some then relatively inexpensive things that we liked, that we could use, and that we could admire and enjoy in our home.

Harriet particularly appreciated the works of Japanese craftsmen of the seventeenth, eighteenth, and nineteenth centuries. The Japan Folk Crafts Museum, near Shibuya, was a stimulating source of information. Among other things, it has a very complete Ōtsu-e collection. Professor Yanagi Sōetsu, the museum's founder, had a great interest in the unknown craftsmen who created works of art for their beauty and not with a desire for personal recognition. He wrote a book on Ōtsu-e, based on the museum's collection, and that book, which we obtained in 1961, contributed substantially to our understanding of these paintings.

Harriet bought our first Ōtsu-e in 1960, from Mr. Yokoi of Mayuyama and Company's shop in the old Imperial Hotel. The painting is of a *takajō*, or falconer (cat. no. 18). Harriet chose it for its strong, confident lines and because she liked looking at it. Before leaving Japan, we purchased several other works, including a *kitsune onna*, or fox woman (cat. no. 15), and a cat and mouse (*neko to nezumi*) drinking *sake* (cat. no. 23), both with moralistic inscriptions.

After returning to Minnesota, we found that we enjoyed our small group of Ōtsu-e more and more, and we began acquiring additional works when we could find them.

Richard Gale, whose Japanese print and painting collection is a highlight of the Asian collections of The Minneapolis Institute of Arts, introduced us to a dealer friend of his, Harry Nail. Harry drove up to see Dick once a year with prints and paintings piled up in the back of his car. From him, in 1968, we purchased a painting of the Buddhist deity Fudō Myō-ō (cat. no. 1). One of the oldest Ōtsu-e in our collection, it probably dates from the mid to late seventeenth century.

Dick also introduced us to Janette Ostier, a Paris dealer who specialized in Japanese crafts, and we bought a number of things from her in the 1960s and 1970s. Most significant is the painting of a courtesan (*tayū*) in a kimono, a wonderfully dramatic work reminiscent of ukiyo-e prints and paintings of similar theme.

By the 1970s we were collecting seriously and looking for paintings to fill gaps in themes and periods. Dealers we purchased from included C. Yamanouchi in Tokyo and Marion Hammer in New York. When Fred Wells opened Asian Fine Arts in Minneapolis in 1980, he searched out Ōtsu-e for us among his dealer contacts in Tokyo and Kyoto. And from Pat Salmon's The Gallery, in Tokyo, came another courtesan, this one wearing a bold plaid kimono (cat. no. 14). Though painted later than the courtesan mentioned above, this figure too has the graceful posture of typical ukiyo-e beauties.

By the mid-1980s, Ōtsu-e were becoming scarcer. We purchased a blind musician with a dog (cat. no. 20) in 1984, from T. Yanagi in Kyoto. For many years after that, however, absolutely nothing came to our attention, despite periodic reminders to dealers in Tokyo and Kyoto that we remained interested. Then just last year, in New York, we stumbled on two marvelous paintings of birds of prey (cat. nos. 21 and 22).

In addition to Ōtsu-e, this catalogue and exhibition include three woodblock prints that show how Ōtsu-e were actually produced in the village of Ōtsu. The print by Hiroshige of a street in Ōtsu (page 6) was given to us by a friend. The triptych and diptych by Kuniyoshi (cat. nos. 25 and 26), showing Matahei drawing Ōtsu-e, were discovered in 1993 in Kyoto.

Looking back, it would be nice to think we had a grand design for building an Ōtsu-e collection. If that had been the case, we would have purchased many more paintings when we lived in Tokyo and they were available. As it was, the collection grew slowly, as did our knowledge and appreciation of the skills of the unnamed artists—peasants who painted religious and humorous themes with refreshing freedom. As the supply of Ōtsu-e dwindled, searching out additions became a good part of the fun of building the collection—and we keep hoping to discover yet another painting from the village of Ōtsu.

Harriet and Ed Spencer

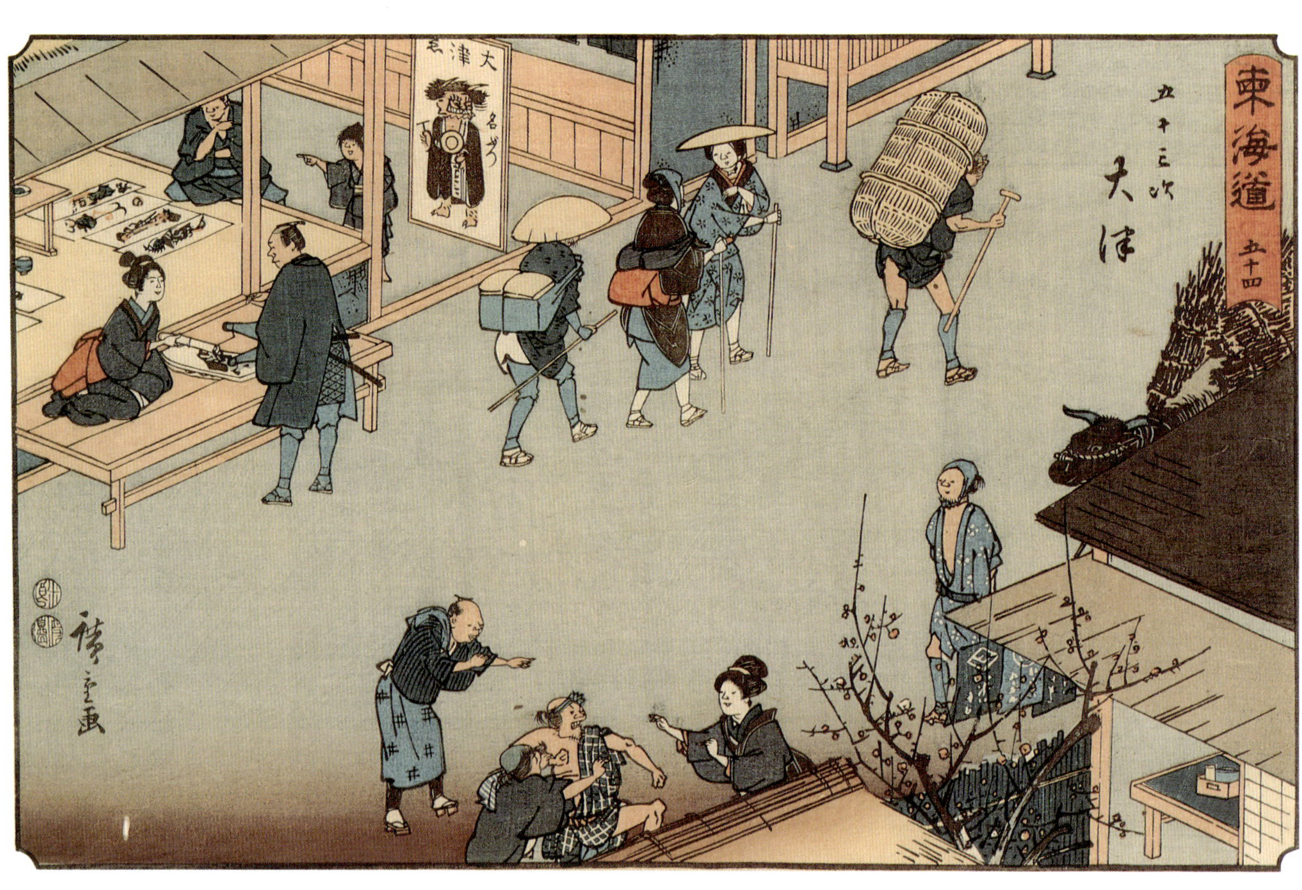

Andō Hiroshige (1797–1858)
Ōtsu, from Tōkaidō series (*reisho* edition), about 1852
Color woodblock print
The Harriet and Edson Spencer Collection

A Historical Overview of Ōtsu-e

Ōtsu-e are folk paintings produced in Japan during the Edo period (1600–1868). These simple images were sold in the shops of Ōtsu, a town on the Tōkaidō roadway just west of the southern tip of Lake Biwa, in Ōmi province (present-day Shiga prefecture). The woodblock print opposite, designed by the renowned artist Andō Hiroshige in the mid-nineteenth century, illustrates a busy street in Ōtsu. Travelers are making their way along the road, some carrying bundles strapped to their backs. A few have stopped at a small shop specializing in local paintings. A large signboard, suspended from the eaves of the building in the upper left corner of the print, displays one of the most popular images—a demon in the guise of a Buddhist priest. One gentleman has just purchased a painting from the shop's proprietress. Another can be seen puzzling over a selection arrayed on the floor for his consideration. And a small boy excitedly gestures toward an unseen painting that has captured his fancy. Barely visible, in the extreme left corner of the print, is a low table on which sits a shallow bowl of paint. The artist is presumably just out of sight, hard at work trying to meet the demands of the constant stream of customers passing through town.

Historical documents also refer to these paintings as Oiwake-e and Otani-e (e meaning picture or painting), after other villages, near Ōtsu, where such paintings were produced. But because Ōtsu was well known as an official way station on the Tōkaidō road—the major route linking the military stronghold of Edo (Tokyo) and the historical capital of Kyoto—all of these paintings came to be known as Ōtsu-e, regardless of their precise place of origin.

Although Ōtsu-e form a distinct stylistic tradition, they share many characteristics with folk painting around the world. They were made by anonymous artists of humble birth with little or no formal artistic training. Unlike professional artists, who aspired to fame and fortune through the creation of unique paintings for a critical, cultured elite, these amateur artists painted images for the common people. Ōtsu-e were mass-produced with inexpensive local materials and sold at prices affordable to all but the poorest. In spite of the repetitiveness of their work (or perhaps because of it), these untrained artists intuitively achieved a spontaneity of touch and compositional balance pleasing to commoner and connoisseur alike.

Obscure Origins

Precisely when the painting of Ōtsu-e began remains a matter of conjecture. The earliest mention in literary documents occurs in the *Jigahō monogatari*, a popular fictional work (*kanazoshi*) written in easily read *kana* syllabary rather than Chinese ideographs. The reference is to an Ōtsu-e of Tenjin being displayed at an amateur poetry gathering[1]—an appropriate image for the occasion, since Tenjin was the deified spirit of Sugawara Michizane (854–903), a court nobleman renowned for his scholarship and poetry. We may reasonably assume that Ōtsu-e were already quite popular by the time the *Jigahō monogatari* was published, in 1661, and that their production preceded this date by at least a decade or two.

Another early reference is found in Hishikawa Moronobu's *Tōkaidō bungen zue* (An Illustrated Map of the Tōkaidō), published in five volumes in 1690. Annotations accompanying a bird's-eye-view drawing of Ōtsu and its surroundings, in the fifth volume, indicate that Buddhist paintings and other goods were sold in that area.[2]

The German physician Englebert Kaempfer (1651–1716), who arrived in Japan in 1690, accompanied a delegation of Dutch merchants on their obligatory journey to Edo for an audience with the shogun and made the following observations about passing through Oiwake:

> A quarter of an hour further we came to Iwanotseja, a small hamlet, and soon after to the large village of Ojiwaki [Oiwake], consisting of one long street of about four hundred houses, inhabited by lock-smiths, turners in wood and ivory, carvers, makers of assiz'd weights, wire-drawers, but particularly painters, and other persons who sell all sorts of Idols and Images.[3]

These literary sources indicate not only that paintings were being produced in the Ōtsu area by the second half of the seventeenth century, but also that their content was religious. The famous haiku poet Matsuo Bashō (1644–94), referring to the variety of sacred paintings in Ōtsu, composed the following lighthearted verse:

Ōtsu-e no fude hajime wa
nani hotoke
What was the first Buddha
painted by the brushes of Ōtsu?[4]

An estimated forty subjects made up the repertoire of early Ōtsu-e artists. Among the most popular was Amida Buddha, prayers to whom could ensure rebirth in the Pure Land of Western Paradise. Another was the bodhisattva Jizō, protector of travelers, women in childbirth, and the souls of dead children. Artists also depicted Shinto and Ryōbu Shintō deities (native gods and native gods as manifestations of Buddhist deities). These included Tenjin, mentioned previously, and Hachiman Bosatsu (the enlightened manifestation of the third-century emperor Ōjin), worshiped as a divine protector. Finally, folk gods such as Ebisu and Daikoku, the "patron saints" of fishermen and farmers respectively, also became subjects for Ōtsu-e, presaging their later popularity. In this exhibition and catalogue, a remarkable painting of Fudō (cat. no. 1), one of the Buddhist Kings of Brightness (Myō-ō), popularly worshiped for protection and courage, represents this early period of Ōtsu-e production.

Artists in Ōtsu

Located near Lake Biwa, on a major thoroughfare, Ōtsu had long been a thriving mercantile center. Fresh produce and fish, gathered from throughout Ōmi province and as far away as the Sea of Japan, were brought by ship across the great lake. From Ōtsu, horses and oxcarts loaded with these goods were dispatched to the metropolis of Kyoto. Why the area around Ōtsu became a center for the production of religious paintings by amateur artists, however, is not readily apparent. Most likely several seemingly unrelated political events created conditions favorable to the development of this unique art form.

The shifting fortunes of Hongan-ji, the head temple of the Jōdo Shin-shū, or True Pure Land, sect of Buddhism ultimately led artists who specialized in Buddhist imagery to migrate to the Ōtsu area.[5]

During the sixteenth century, the sect's headquarters, called Ishiyama Hongan-ji, was located near Osaka Bay. With devoted followers throughout the country, Ishiyama Hongan-ji garnered considerable wealth and power. During its heyday, innumerable people from far and wide made pilgrimages to Hongan-ji. Outside the temple, a marketplace grew up that catered to the needs of these pious visitors, supplying them with devotional paintings and ritual Buddhist implements, which they purchased and carried back home.

The temple itself was heavily fortified and protected by militant monks and countless lay followers, from high-ranking warlords to ordinary peasants. The abbot of Hongan-ji, who was related by marriage to the ruling shogun, vehemently opposed the upstart general Oda Nobunaga (1534–82), who was attempting to unite the country under his own dominion. But after a decade of repeated attacks by Nobunaga, the temple surrendered in 1580.

Toyotomi Hideyoshi, Oda Nobunaga's successor, was less ill-disposed toward the adherents of the Shin sect. Nevertheless, he recognized the potential danger of allowing them to reestablish their headquarters in the garrisoned stronghold of Ishiyama. Hideyoshi replaced the chief abbot, Kyōnyo Kōju (1558–1614), who had resisted Nobunaga, with Kōju's brother Junnyo Kōshō (1577–1631). And he allowed the new abbot to begin building a temple, also known as Hongan-ji, in the southern section of Kyoto. The artisans who had occupied the marketplace at Ishiyama Hongan-ji were encouraged to come to Kyoto and set up their businesses in the area outside the great gate of the new temple.

To counter the still-growing power of the temple, the next shogun, Tokugawa Ieyasu, sponsored the construction of yet another temple and appointed the deposed priest Kōju as abbot, thus dividing the loyalties of the Shin sect. Located near Hongan-ji, the new temple was known as Higashi Hongan-ji, or Eastern Hongan-ji. To make way for it, the recently reestablished marketplace had to be moved yet again. Under a government order issued in 1602, some of the merchants, including needle and abacus makers and Buddhist painters, relocated to the Ōtsu area. Thus, even by the early years of the seventeenth century, there was a contingent of Buddhist painters in the vicinity of Ōtsu.

The forced move away from the metropolitan temples in Kyoto did not necessarily cause the artists and craftsmen financial hardship. Ōtsu was a thriving commercial center, and its situation on the Tōkaidō roadway assured

Ōtsu-e painters of numerous customers daily. As the most direct and easily traversed route linking the shogun's military stronghold in Edo with the major cities to the west, the Tōkaidō was heavily traveled. And since Ōtsu was located south of where the Kisokaidō roadway joined the Tōkaidō, most travelers from the east, whether they took the Tōkaidō along the Pacific coast or the Kisokaidō through the central mountains, passed through Ōtsu before arriving in Kyoto.

Traffic on the road increased substantially during the early decades of the seventeenth century, partly because of economic prosperity and brisk mercantile activity and partly owing to the requirement of "alternate attendance," or *sankin kōtai*. Under this system, the daimyo (feudal lords) had to spend alternate years in Edo, ostensibly to serve at the shogun's court. In reality, the system was cleverly devised to keep the fortunes and power of the daimyo in check. Each feudal lord wasted a good deal of time traveling from his domain to Edo and then back again. In Edo, he was required to maintain a residence commensurate with his status, a huge drain on his income. When he returned to his domain, his family stayed in Edo, guaranteeing that he would make no hostile moves against the shogun. This policy put many more travelers on Japan's roadways. With over two hundred and thirty daimyo at any given time, each with a different period of attendance in order to stagger their presence in Edo, daimyo processions were a common sight. Depending upon the lord's rank and status, his entourage could number in the thousands. The fifty-three "stations" of the Tōkaidō, including Ōtsu, were established to cater to the needs of these official travelers.

Proof of Piety

Another political development that ultimately had a great effect on the production of Buddhist painting in Ōtsu was the governmental policy toward Christianity.[6] Jesuit missionaries, who first arrived in Japan with Portuguese trading merchants in the mid-sixteenth century, had enjoyed considerable success in their early efforts to introduce their faith to the Japanese people. The warlord Oda Nobunaga, in particular, seems to have been favorably disposed toward the missionaries, probably more out of distaste for the political machinations of militant Buddhist monks than from any true faith.[7]

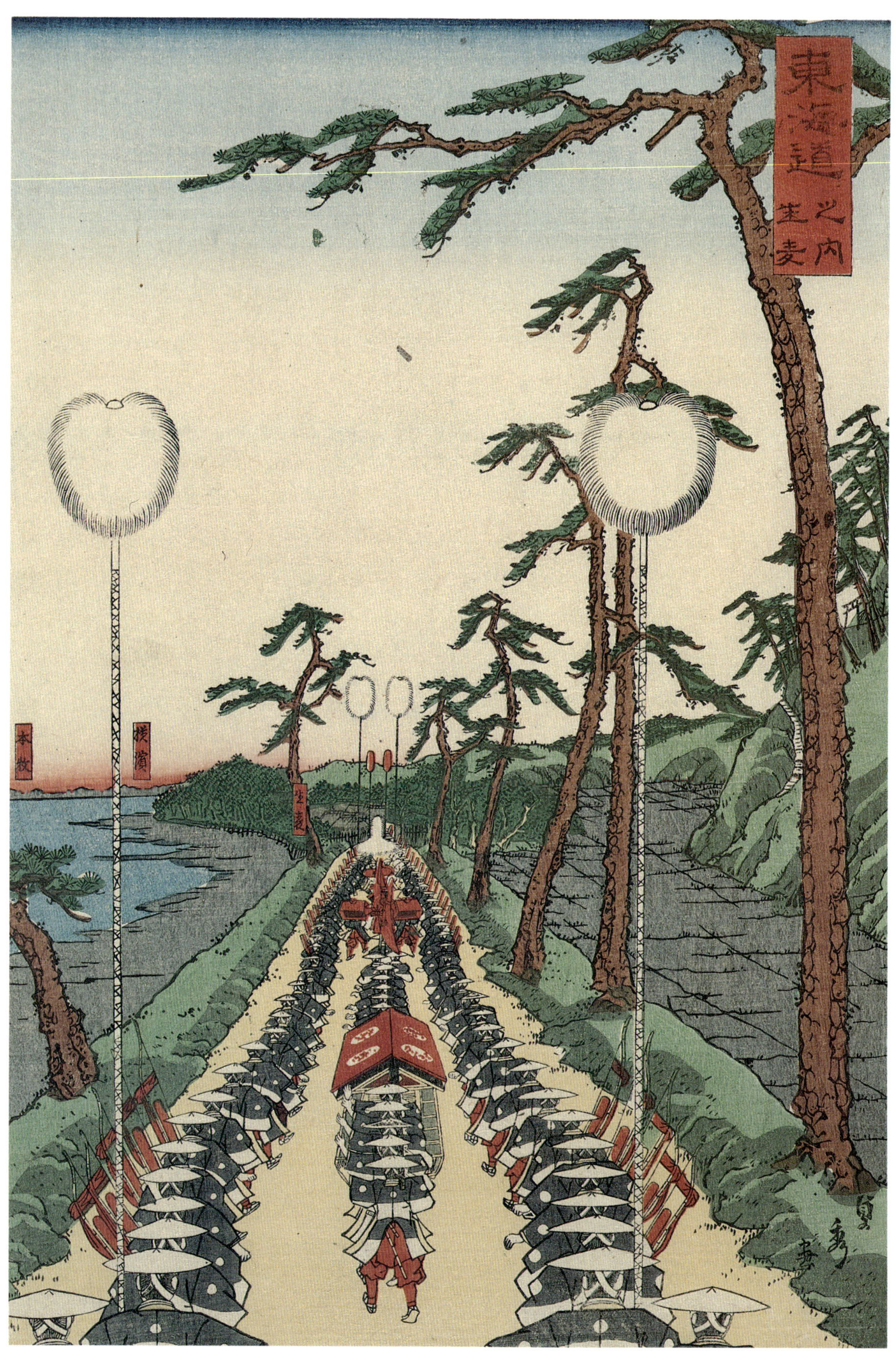
東海道之内
生麦
本牧
横濱

Nobunaga's successor, Toyotomi Hideyoshi, however, was distrustful of the Jesuits and concerned by the growing number of faithful followers. He probably viewed the Jesuits' presence in Japan as a prelude to Spanish and Portuguese imperialism and thus a threat to the sovereignty of Japan and to his own authority. In 1587, he issued an edict summarily banning Christianity and ordering the priests to leave the country. Evading this command and taking the movement underground, the faithful continued to proselytize, gaining converts among both commoners and high-ranking warrior families. By 1595 there were reportedly more than 140 Jesuit priests in Japan and over 300,000 Japanese Christians. Hideyoshi probably neglected to enforce his edict only because he was preoccupied with the conquest of Korea and the question of succession.[8]

The next shogun, Tokugawa Ieyasu, and his successors, Hidetada and Iemitsu, made more determined efforts to limit foreign influence in Japan. As part of a broader seclusionist policy, they began in 1611 to issue edicts banning Christianity. Those who refused to renounce the heretical religion were brutally tortured and crucified. Resorting to near maniacal methods of ferreting out "hidden" Christians, the government required that every citizen be registered at a Buddhist temple of an accepted sect and that these parishioners proclaim their faith in Buddhism annually. From 1641, government officials began conducting further tests of faith, requiring suspected Christians to trample upon images of the Virgin Mary or Christ (*fumi-e*). Those who resisted were judged guilty and arrested. Japanese lived in dread of incurring the suspicion of the government censors who traveled house to house severely questioning people about their beliefs. Handsome rewards were offered to those who reported their neighbors. Claiming adherence to Buddhism was not enough; people had to prove they were not Christian. One way of doing so was to display a Buddhist painting in their homes.[9]

Naturally the demand for Buddhist imagery rose dramatically as the government stepped up its search for secret Christians. Commoners, unable to purchase expensive paintings by professional Buddhist artists, turned to a rising

Utagawa Sadahide (1807–73)
Namamugi, from Tōkaidō series, 1863
Color woodblock print
The Minneapolis Institute of Arts, gift of an anonymous St. Paul friend

group of amateur painters who reproduced professionally painted works as best they could. The Ōtsu area, already a center of professional Buddhist painting, became a hub of amateur Buddhist painting as well.

As the government's efforts to track down Christians intensified, painters were hard pressed to keep up with demand. Amateur Buddhist painters in the Ōtsu area used several strategies to speed production. They simplified artistic compositions and abbreviated the overall rendering of Buddhist images. Where professional painters took considerable pride in the elegance and precision of their brushwork, amateur artists wielded their brushes hastily, substituting frenzied bravura for careful accuracy. To speed production even more, they employed simple stencils cut from heavy paper. Using a brush, they applied pigments through the stencil, blocking in large areas of color. Then, with brush and ink, they quickly rendered faces, hands, and simplified drapery folds. Rather than trusting their skill with the brush, these artists commonly used compasses to draw the circular halos surrounding Buddhist deities and a straightedge when painting the rays of light emanating from their bodies. Certain details were carved on small woodblock stamps, so they could be rapidly impressed rather than painted. The faces of Buddhist deities, particularly the attendant figures in Buddhist triads, were often accomplished by this time-saving method.[10]

Unlike professional painters, who used a wide range of expensive materials, amateur artists were limited to the pigments and paper available locally. They used rough paper, possibly even the low-quality stock used to back expensive paintings on silk.[11] To create a smoother surface, necessary for obtaining crisp results from a stencil, they brushed onto this rough paper a thin layer of *ōdo*, a pale clay. Their restricted range of pigments was mostly derived from common materials. For the gold leaf and gold powder applied by professional artists to suggest the divinity and otherworldly splendor of Buddhist deities, amateur artists substituted brass filings. Instead of bordering their images with precious fragments of silk brocade to create a sumptuous hanging scroll, the early amateur painters purposely confined their images to the center of the paper and painted the surrounding area to resemble a fabric mounting. Then they attached bamboo dowels to the top and bottom of the painting and secured a string to the top dowel. Thus the painting was ready for hanging without the extra expense of enlisting the services of a professional mounter.[12]

In rapidly producing these paintings to meet the high demand for images of Buddhist and Ryōbu Shintō deities, amateur artists unconsciously evolved a style that distinguished their works from mere hack copies of professional paintings. Their limited palette, roughly applied with stencils, produced strikingly dramatic results. Their brushwork, for all its repetition and recklessness, was pleasingly casual, even exciting. It was precisely this freedom and spontaneity, arrived at intuitively through constant repetition rather than conscious effort, that became the hallmark of Ōtsu-e.[13]

Earthly Delights

The final decades of the seventeenth century saw a shift in the types of images painted by Ōtsu-e artists. Previously, religious themes had dominated, but now secular subjects became increasingly common. To be sure, images of the most popular religious deities continued to be painted, but by the early eighteenth century, Ōtsu-e had undergone a radical transformation both in content and in tone.

The decline of religious Ōtsu-e probably reflected a drop in demand. Although the Tokugawa government strictly maintained its policy against Christianity, by the 1670s or 1680s other matters had begun to claim its attention. As the pressing need to display evidence of Buddhist faith diminished, the clamor to purchase religious Ōtsu-e likely abated.

The rise of secular Ōtsu-e with jocular, even satirical, themes reflected the tenor of the times. Their production coincided with the Genroku era (1688–1704), a period of Japanese history characterized by the flourishing of plebian culture. The peace that prevailed under the stern rule of the Tokugawa shogunate fostered the rapid growth of urban centers—most notably Kyoto, Osaka, and Edo (Tokyo)—and merchants and artisans grew rich providing goods and services for the inhabitants of these bustling cities. The strict stratification of Japanese society prevented these prosperous townsmen (known as *chōnin*) from advancing socially, in spite of their wealth. As a result, they pursued a hedonistic lifestyle, indulging in extravagant pastimes. By the middle of the seventeenth century, *chōnin* constituted a dynamic cultural force capable of engendering art forms suited to their own needs and tastes. Kabuki theater and puppet performances, for example, were increasingly staged for the amusement of *chōnin* audiences.

The Genroku era also saw the rapid development of popular literature which, in the hands of writers like Ihara Saikaku (1642–93) and Asai Ryōi (died 1691), focused on contemporary society, particularly the dalliances and intrigues of the townsmen themselves. In addition to illustrated books, a new style of painting and woodblock print design emerged, known as ukiyo-e, or pictures of the floating world. Although famous actors and legendary women of the licensed pleasure quarters were their most common subjects, ukiyo-e artists produced an endless variety of designs to satisfy the *chōnin*'s voracious appetite for anything new and delightful.

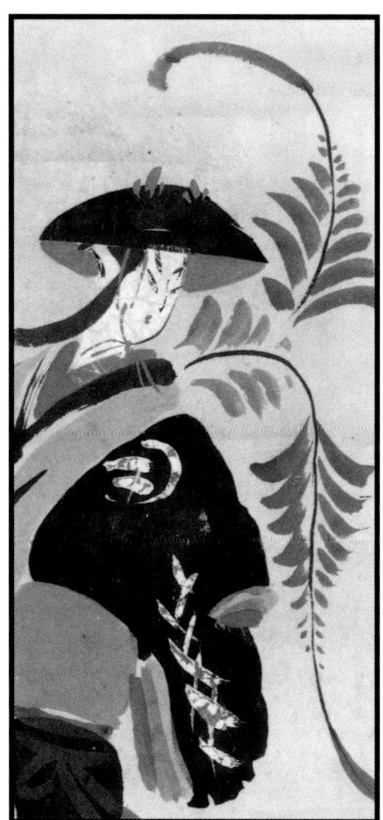

Detail, cat. no. 12

Responding to the expansive tastes of their plebian customers, Ōtsu-e artists not only turned to secular themes, but also greatly enlarged their repertoire. Many subjects were directly inspired by ukiyo-e. Ōtsu-e artists painted lively renditions of high-ranking courtesans clothed in sumptuous robes (cat. nos. 13 and 14). They copied the distinctive, alluring poses of these women and produced simplified versions of such standard ukiyo-e images as a beauty reading a love letter, strolling with an umbrella, and playing a *shamisen* (cat. no. 15). Nevertheless, the most frequently painted Ōtsu-e beauty of all, the wisteria maiden, owed her popularity less to the influence of ukiyo-e than to the Ōtsu-e artists' free and exuberant rendering of the wisteria spray as great abstract arabesques (cat. no. 12).

Ōtsu-e artists also found inspiration in the bustling world around them. The great daimyo processions that passed through Ōtsu and Oiwake provided several themes, such as the spear bearers (cat. no. 16). Holding their tall, fur- and feathered-sheathed spears upright, these robust foot soldiers signaled people to clear the road. Other subjects derived from the daimyo procession included handsome young samurai, falconers (cat. nos. 17 and 18), and even lowly porters.

Legendary heroes from Japan's distant past, resurrected on the Kabuki stage, also entered the repertoire of Ōtsu-e artists. The most popular may have been Benkei, a warrior-monk of the twelfth century renowned for his great size and martial skills. Two of Benkei's well-known exploits, stealing the temple bell of Miidera (cat. no. 11) and defending his master Yoshitsune at the battle of Koromogawa (cat. no. 10), became popular Ōtsu-e themes.

The simple compositions and informal style of Ōtsu-e painters made their works seem playful whatever the content. Some themes, however, were intentionally humorous. For example, Daikoku, the god of abundance, was depicted fretfully shaving the elongated head of Fukurokuju, the god of longevity (cat. nos. 5 and 6). The god of thunder, instead of riding majestically atop ominous storm clouds, was shown frantically trying to retrieve his thunder-making drum, which he had accidentally dropped into the sea (cat. no. 8). In both cases, humor arises from the mild irreverence implicit in presenting these minor deities as unlucky victims of the same concerns and mishaps that plague mortals. In other cases, the humor is tinged with a bit of satire. An *oni*, a kind of impish demon, masquerading as a Buddhist monk, playfully suggests the devilish nature of a corrupt clergy (cat. no. 7). A bushy tail protruding from the hem of a beautiful woman's kimono indicates that she is actually a mischievous fox (or a fickle woman) in disguise, hoping to hoodwink unsuspecting men (cat. no. 15).

With the development of secular themes, the popularity of Ōtsu-e seems to have risen dramatically. When Ōtsu-e production was at its height, customers could choose from an astonishingly large repertoire, estimated at some 340 different subjects.[14] Following the precedent set by early painters of religious Ōtsu-e, artists created simplified compositions with abbreviated brushwork and a limited palette of pigments applied with stencils. But unlike the early painters, who had adopted these techniques out of necessity, to meet the high demand for religious images, the artists of Ōtsu-e's "golden age" purposely capitalized on the naïve charm of this informal painting style. Freed from the need to make images of solemn deities, they matched their animated brushwork with suitably lighthearted and dramatic subjects. As a result, Ōtsu-e from the early decades of the eighteenth century are among the most expressively rendered of all.

Unconcerned with producing ready-made hanging scrolls, artists dispensed with painted mountings. Whereas early Ōtsu-e often consisted of three or four pieces of paper pasted together to create a large composition, in imitation of Buddhist painting, by the early eighteenth century Ōtsu-e had been reduced to the more manageable size of two sheets, glued together to form a vertical composition roughly twenty-four by nine inches. The subject matter, boldly and rapidly delineated in dark ink, was expanded to fill the surface of the paper. In a painting from this period of Benkei with a halberd (cat. no. 10), Benkei seems barely contained by the confines of the paper.

Yet for all its creative vitality, Ōtsu-e remained essentially a folk art, painted by anonymous artists working with humble materials. Compositions were kept deliberately simple, usually focusing on a single figure isolated on the paper, with no attempt to articulate a background setting. Once established, the new themes were mass-produced with little variation. For example, while images of falconers show the touch of individual artists, they invariably follow the basic formula of a standing youth, with a bird perched on his left arm, striding to the right while looking back to the left (cat. nos. 17 and 18). In this respect Ōtsu-e differ sharply from the prints and paintings of ukiyo-e artists, who rendered the human figure in countless poses, often within an elaborate architectural or landscape setting.

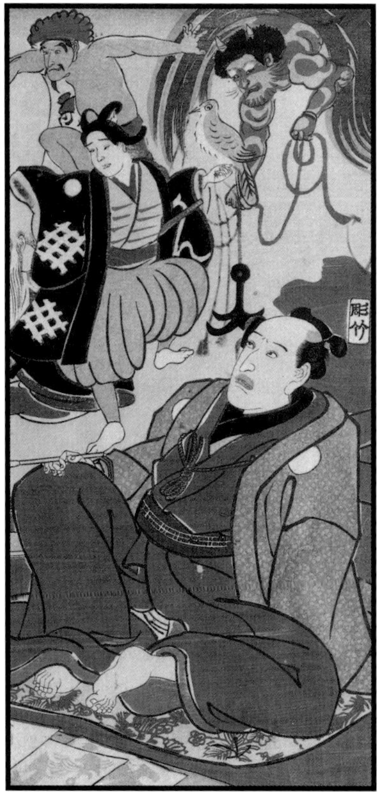
Detail, cat. no. 26

Innumerable travelers purchased paintings while passing through Ōtsu, and these simple works of art became well known throughout Japan. In 1708 the famed playwright of the puppet theater (*jōruri*) Chikamatsu Monzaemon (1653– 1724) wrote a play, entitled *Keisei hangonkō* (The Beauty Whose Spirit Appears in the Incense Smoke), that featured a painter of Ōtsu-e in one of its many subplots. Known as Ukiyo Matahei, this artist was a young pupil of Tosa Shōgen. Although born to a poor family and suffering a speech impediment, Matahei excelled at painting. So great was his talent, the story goes, that Shōgen adopted Matahei as an heir to his painting tradition.[15]

Two episodes in the play serve to establish the rare talents of Matahei. In the first, the subjects of his paintings magically come to life and protect him when he is about to be arrested. Matahei's brushwork was so vigorous, it seems, that the characters literally leapt from the paper. In another scene, he paints a self-portrait on the side of a stone water-basin. So forceful was the touch of his brush that his image appeared on the other side of the stone.[16]

Chikamatsu's liberal borrowing of the names of actual artists from the past lent his fiction an air of historical truth. An artist known as Iwasa Matabei

(1578–1650), for example, had produced genre paintings in the early seventeenth century which were a hybrid of Tosa and Kanō school styles, presaging the development of ukiyo-e. In creating the character of Matahei, Chikamatsu clearly hoped to capitalize on the popular interest in the pivotal artist Matabei. Similarly, the fictional character Tosa Shōgen is a conflation of the actual artists Tosa Mitsunobu (1435– 1525), a painter of colorful, minutely detailed Japanese subjects, and Kanō Masanobu (1434–1530), famous for his Chinese-inspired painting style. Masanobu's art alias, incidentally, was Shōgen.

In any case, by creating a mythical originator of Ōtsu-e in the form of Matahei, whose identity quickly became confused in people's minds with actual artists, Chikamatsu likely fostered a new respect and admiration for these simple paintings and contributed to their continuing popularity. Certainly the myth of Matahei endured; in the mid-nineteenth century, the ukiyo-e artist Utagawa Kuniyoshi (1797–1861) designed woodblock prints based on Chikamatsu's play (cat. nos. 25 and 26).

Studies of the Heart

The next major development in Ōtsu-e was related to the spread of a quasi-religious movement known as Shingaku, "studies of the heart." Formulated by Ishida Baigan (1685–1744), son of a peasant farmer, Shingaku was a popular form of Confucianism, which attached religious significance to ethical conduct. It originated in Kyoto and, propagated by Baigan's followers Tejima Toan (1718–86) and Nakazawa Dōni (1725–1803), quickly gained converts and supporters throughout the country.

In its essential form, Shingaku equated spiritual awakening, through circumspection and meditation, with an understanding and acceptance of morality. Baigan held that the merchant class, in pursuing profit, was merely fulfilling its destiny—a destiny no less honorable than that of the noble samurai class, providing the merchant was fair in business and used his profits responsibly and charitably. According to Baigan, merchants ought to be content with their lot and live frugally and honestly, and in so doing they would preserve universal harmony.[17] In legitimizing the merchant's role in society, Shingaku fostered a sense of dignity and collective identity among a class traditionally viewed as parasitic—as profiting from the traffic of commodities while producing nothing themselves.

During the last half of the eighteenth century, Ōtsu-e began to reflect Shingaku teachings.[18] Simple verses consisting of moral lessons, exhortations to lead a virtuous life, or observations on the corruptness of human nature began to appear on Ōtsu-e (cat. nos. 2, 4, 15, 16, and 23). A verse written on a painting of Amida Buddha, for example, says that rather than fashioning images from clay, wood, metal, or stone we should mold ourselves to the Buddha nature (cat. no. 2). And a humorous painting of a cat plying a mouse with *sake* carries a verse cautioning against the dangers of carelessness and, by extension, of indulgence in drink (cat. no. 23). Rapidly written, usually in the easily read *kana* syllabary, such verses complemented the casual quality of the painting. Often several were added to a single painting, filling the areas around the image. When *kanji* (Chinese characters) were used, *furigana* (phonetic transcriptions in *kana*) were included to ensure that even the least literate could grasp the meaning.

At the same time that Shingaku verses appeared on Ōtsu-e, the size of the paintings changed. A single sheet of paper, roughly twelve by nine inches, replaced the double-sheet vertical compositions of the golden age. The figures, too, became smaller and, although charming, were rendered with much less gusto.

Ironically, as Ōtsu-e began to decline, a guild of Ōtsu-e painters was established and some artists began to sign their works. Many of the names, such as Tosa Mataheiji and Mantei Matahei, derived from the legendary Matahei. Nevertheless, these painters do not seem to have achieved individual fame, and nothing is known of their lives.[19]

Fanciful Talismans

By the early nineteenth century, the once flourishing Ōtsu-e tradition was declining. From guidebooks and woodblock prints showing roadside shops in Ōtsu and Oiwake, it is clear that Ōtsu-e continued to be produced and sold to travelers along the Tōkaidō. But later artists never managed to re-create the brilliantly unconstrained brushwork that had characterized the golden age of Ōtsu-e. Their paintings were small in scale, and the increasingly doll-like Ōtsu-e characters lacked the expansive presence of earlier renderings. Most notable, however, was the radical reduction of themes. After 1800, a mere ten subjects constituted the entire Ōtsu-e repertoire.[20]

Perhaps because of the concentration on a few themes, talismanic powers came to be associated with Ōtsu-e. A painting of a demon chanting Buddhist invocations (*oni no nembutsu*) was purchased in the belief that it would prevent a baby from crying at night. The wisteria maiden (*fuji musume*) could help secure a good marriage, and the falconer (*takajō*) helped ensure a bountiful harvest.[21] In many respects, the efficacious powers ascribed to these paintings were similar to those associated with the charms and amulets (*omamori*) traditionally distributed by temples and shrines.

Although Ōtsu-e degenerated artistically to near lifelessness, their widespread distribution over a long period of time assured them a place in the collective Japanese psyche. Many popular songs and performances featured Ōtsu-e subjects and the legend of Matahei. A dance performed at the Nakamura-za Kabuki theater in Edo in 1826, for example, was called "Fuji musume" (Wisteria Maiden), presumably after the Ōtsu-e character of that name—a beautiful woman carrying a wisteria branch over her shoulder.[22]

Ōtsu-e characters also became subjects for print designers and painters. A drawing attributed to Katsushika Hokusai (1760–1849) illustrating the god of

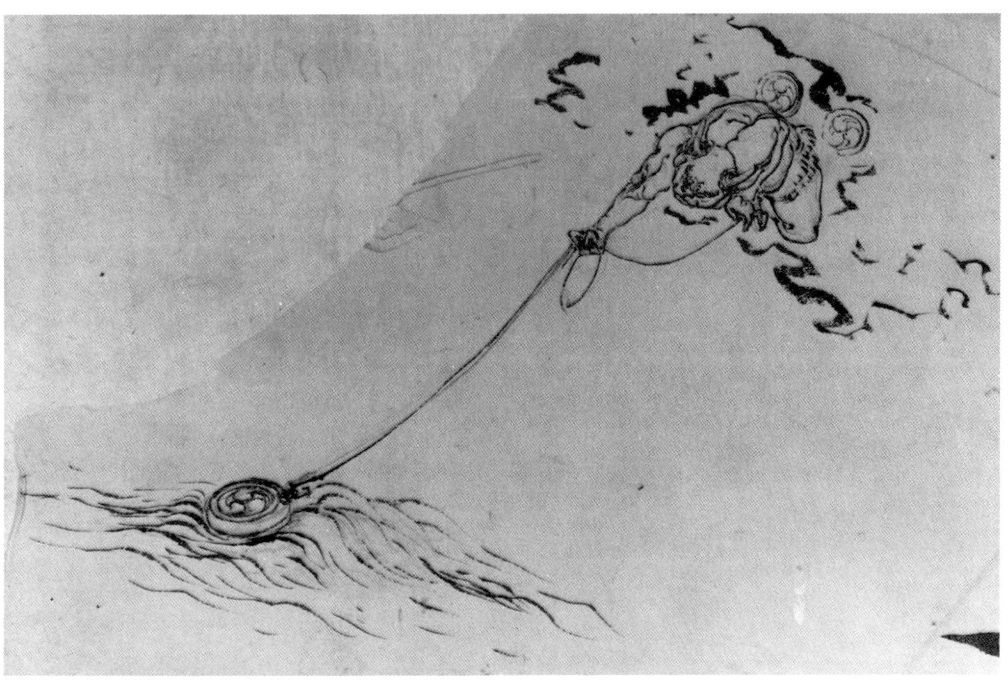

Attributed to Katsushika Hokusai (1760–1849)
God of Thunder and His Drum
Sketchbook; ink on paper
The Minneapolis Institute of Arts

thunder frantically fishing for his drum, which he has accidentally dropped into the sea, is clearly based on Ōtsu-e of the same theme. Kitagawa Utamaro (1754–1806) designed at least two woodblock prints entitled *Edo shii Ōtsu miyage* (Souvenirs of Ōtsu Available in Edo). In one, a robust spear bearer, rendered in imitation of the Ōtsu-e artists' rough brushwork, is juxtaposed with an elegant falconer in ukiyo-e style. In another, the wisteria maiden, depicted with the crisp precision of ukiyo-e, is shown with an Ōtsu-e–style demon masquerading as a Buddhist priest.[23] In a creative attempt to circumvent government strictures against depicting members of the ruling family and Kabuki actors, Utagawa Kuniyoshi (1797– 1861) cleverly disguised his portraits as Ōtsu-e characters in woodblock prints that ostensibly represent the legend of Matahei (cat. nos. 25 and 26).

Artists from other schools, too, borrowed Ōtsu-e themes. Kawanabe Kyōsai (1831–89), a late Kanō school painter, playfully depicted Ōtsu-e characters in a woodblock book, *Kyōsai hyakuzu*, published in 1881. One illustration shows them as travelers fording the Oigawa with Mount Fuji in the background: the wisteria maiden is carried by the blind minstrel; the falconer rides on the shoulders of a demon; and Daikoku, the god of abundance, perches atop the tall head of Fukurokuju, the god of longevity. Another page from the same book shows the spear bearer, demon, god of longevity, and god of abundance engaged in contests of

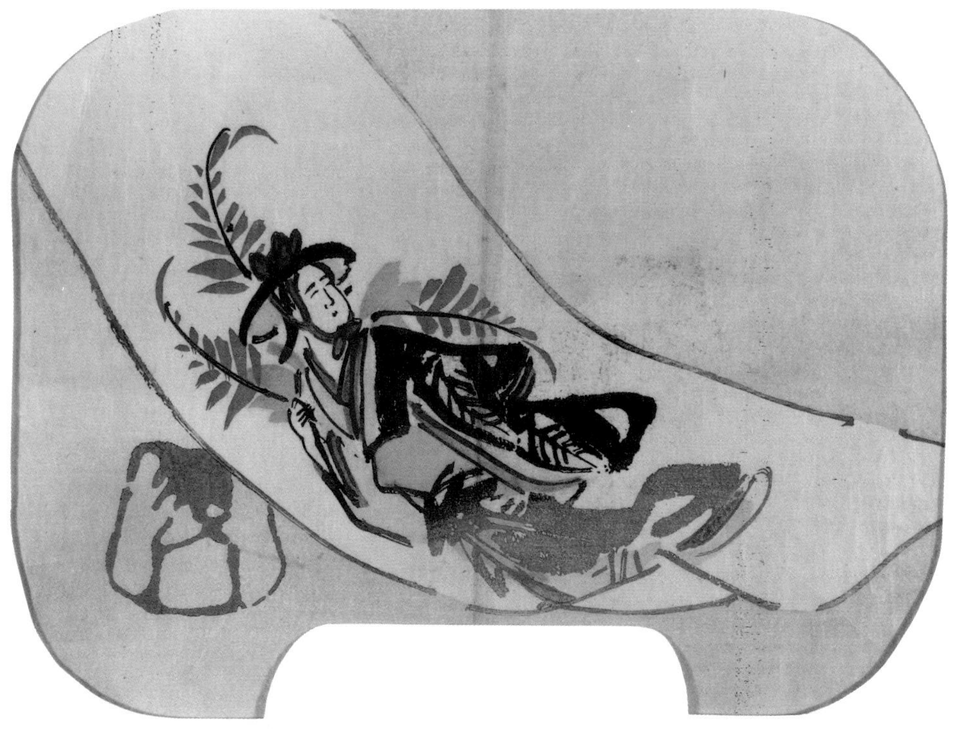

strength.[24] Other artists simply enjoyed the original informality and roughness of Ōtsu-e and were content to reproduce this style with little alteration. The Shijō school artist Yamada Hōgyoku (active about 1840), for instance, borrowed the wisteria maiden for a printed fan design. Only in the slight softening of the outlines and colors is Hōgyoku's own artistic pedigree evident.

When Hiroshige produced his woodblock design showing a street in Ōtsu with a small shop selling distinctive folk paintings, Japan was on the verge of cataclysmic change. Within a few years, Commodore Matthew Perry sailed his black battleships into the port of Uraga to forcibly deliver a letter from President Fillmore to Tokugawa Iesada, the supreme military leader who ruled Japan in the name of the emperor. A veiled threat, the letter requested that Japan end its policy of seclusion, enforced for over two hundred years, and open itself to foreign trade. The signing of a treaty with the United States in 1854, followed by similar agreements with England, Russia, France, and Holland, suddenly exposed Japan to the advanced technologies of these industrialized nations. In just a few decades, railroads were built, telegraph lines installed, and a postal service opened; a host of political and financial reforms were initiated based on Western models. Many traditional arts, long enjoyed by the Japanese, were abandoned as the country embarked on an ambitious program of modernization.

Hiroshige's peaceful scene of Ōtsu illustrates a way of life that was destined to change. People soon ceased traveling the Tōkaidō by foot. Forgotten were the simple pleasures of such a slow and arduous journey: the breathtaking scenery, a skillful massage at an inn after a long, dusty day, and the local products and souvenirs purchased by the way. The gradual closing of the painting shops of Ōtsu brought an end to a long and lively artistic tradition. Ōtsu-e remain a testimony to the breadth of Japanese aesthetic appreciation, which embraces not only the refined and beautiful, but also the simple, rough, and intuitive paintings of anonymous artists.

Yamada Hōgyoku (active about 1840)
Wisteria Maiden
Color woodblock fan print
The Minneapolis Institute of Arts, gift of an anonymous St. Paul friend

Notes

1. Ono Tadashige, "Ōtsu-e kō," in *Kaidō ni umarete minga: Ōtsu-e* (Kyoto: Korin-sha, 1991), p. 225.

2. Ibid.

3. Englebert Kaempfer, *The History of Japan together with a Description of the Kingdom of Siam, 1690–92*, trans. J. G. Scheuchzer (Glasgow, 1906), 3:26.

4. Ono, p. 225.

5. The following information about the marketplace painters assoicated with Hongan-ji is taken from Makioka Ashihei, "Ōtsu-e o kanzuru mikata," in *Kaidō ni umarete minga: Ōtsu-e* (Kyoto: Korin-sha, 1991), pp. 269–70.

6. Ibid., p. 270.

7. George Sansom, *A History of Japan, 1334–1615* (1961; reprint, Stanford, Calif.: Stanford University Press, 1987), p. 295.

8. Ibid., pp. 347–50.

9. Ono, p. 226.

10. See Tokuriki Tomiyoshirō, "Ōtsu-e no gihō," in *Kaidō ni umarete minga: Ōtsu-e* (Kyoto: Korin-sha, 1991), pp. 277–80.

11. Ibid., p. 280. Tokuriki points out that there have been many theories and assumptions about the kinds of paper used in the production of Ōtsu-e. He concludes that the paper must have been produced locally, probably in Kyoto.

12. Ibid., pp. 277–80.

13. Makioka, pp. 270–71.

14. Ono, p. 234.

15. Samuel L. Leiter, *Kabuki Encyclopedia: An English-Language Adaptation of Kabuki Jiten* (Westport, Conn.: Greenwood Press, 1979), p. 188.

16. Ibid.

17. Robert N. Bellah, *Tokugawa Religion* (Boston: Beacon Press, 1957), pp. 133–77.

18. Ono, p. 238.

19. Ibid., p. 239.

20. Ibid.

21. Ibid.

22. Kobayashi Tadashi, *Ōtsu-e* (Machida: Machida Municipal Museum, 1990), p. 54.

23. *Tokyo Kokuritsu Hakubutsukan zuhan mokuroku: Ukiyo-e hanga hen* (Tokyo: Tokyo Kokuritsu Hakubutsukan, 1974), vol. 2, pls. 2046, 2047.

24. Kawanabe Kusumi et al., *Botsugo hyakunen kinen tokubetsuten: Kawanabe Kyōsai ten* (Tokyo: Ota Kinen Bijutsukan, 1989), pl. 184.

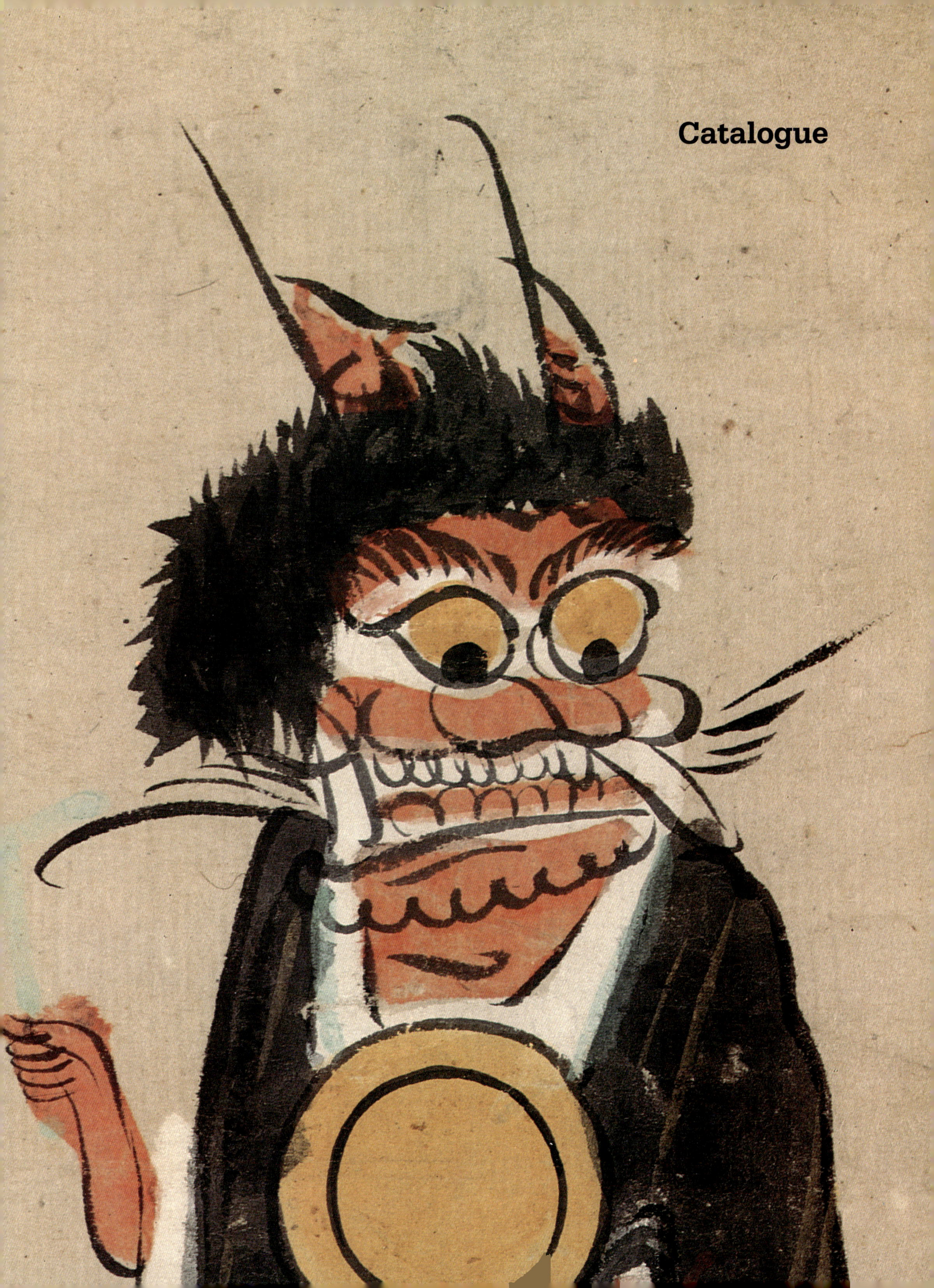

Catalogue

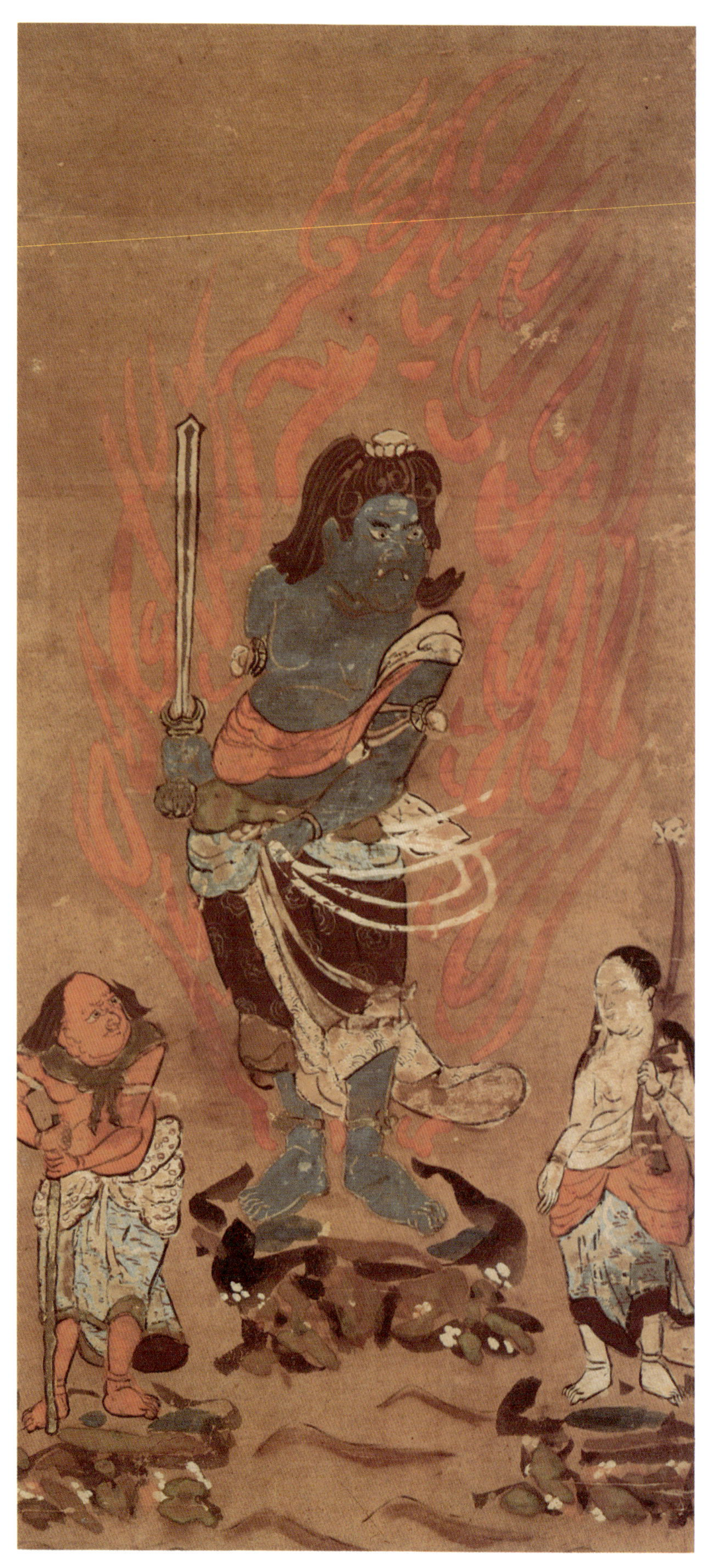

1

Fudō Myō-ō

17th century

Hanging scroll; ink and colors on paper

20 9/16 × 9 9/16 inches

Known as Acala in Sanskrit, Fudō was originally a manifestation of Shiva, the Hindu god of destruction. Adopted into the Buddhist pantheon, he became the most important of the five Myō-ō, or Kings of Brightness. In contrast to bodhisattvas, who are heavenly beings of infinite grace and compassion, Myō-ō are wrathful deities devoted to protecting the Buddhist truth. They are usually depicted as ferocious beings with strange and frightening attributes. In traditional iconography, Fudō has blue skin and fangs that grow in opposite directions. His hair is bound in a single plait and hangs down over his left shoulder. He carries the Sword of Wisdom, with which he defeats evil and slashes deluded thought, and a rope, which he uses to tie demons and lasso floundering souls, pulling them to salvation. Associated with fire, he stands amid purifying flames, usually represented by a flaming mandorla. Because he is steadfast in his resolve and unyielding before all obstacles, his name literally means "the Immovable." This quality is also suggested by his firm stance and heavy musculature and by the rocky pedestal on which he stands. Fudō is usually accompanied by two child attendants, the white-skinned Kongara and the red-skinned Seitaka.

Although frightening in appearance, Fudō is essentially benevolent in his commitment to the salvation of all sentient beings. One of the many deities brought to Japan with esoteric Buddhism in the ninth century, Fudō gained general popularity during the Edo period (1600–1868). People prayed to Fudō for protection from evil and for courage in the face of hardship. Mountain ascetics known as *yamabushi* were also devoted to Fudō and, in an attempt to acquire his miraculous powers, would perform various rites of purification, such as standing beneath the frigid torrents of a waterfall or walking on smoldering embers.[1]

Given the popularity of this awe-inspiring deity, it is not surprising that paintings of Fudō are to be found among surviving Ōtsu-e. This scroll dates to the earliest period of Ōtsu-e production, when Buddhist imagery predominated. The artist took great care to follow iconographic precedents and included most of the characteristics associated with Fudō. Compared with other Ōtsu-e of Fudō, this one is finely painted. The scarves and skirts of the deity and his attendants are outlined with relatively fine lines and decorated with various delicate patterns in gold. Yet the rough, exuberant brushwork typical of Ōtsu-e is used to great effect for the raging flames that surround Fudō.

1. Ian Reader, *Religion in Contemporary Japan* (Honolulu: University of Hawaii Press, 1991), p. 118.

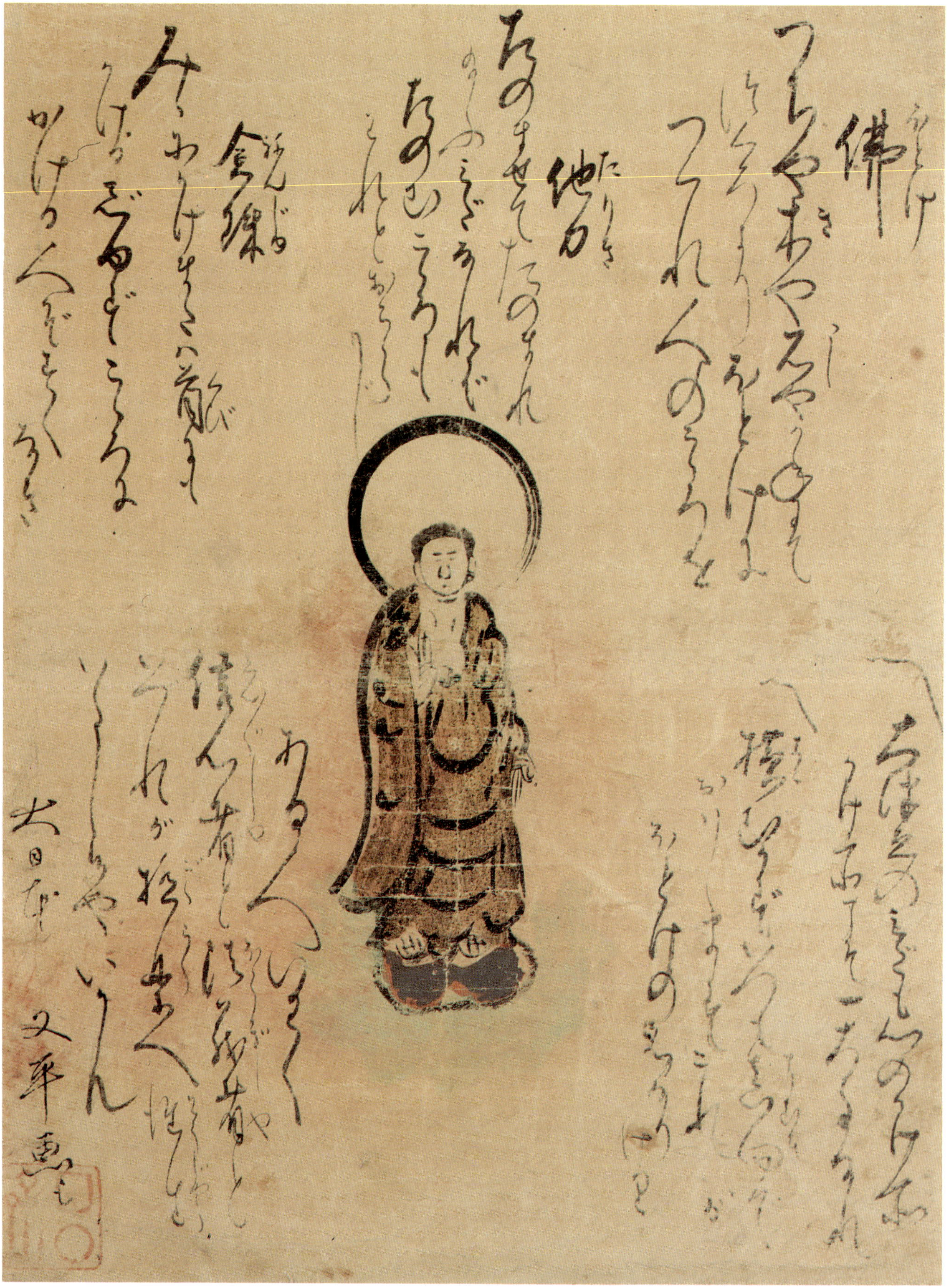

佛（ほとけ）
つらやおやゑやうゆすし
はらえりきよけよ
つられ人のこころを

他力（たりき）
たのませてたのまれ
のりかえざるれど
たのむこころし
これとしおもふし

金縛（かんじがらみ）
みなわけすきへ論（ろんじ）まて
けがるぞこころみ
かけつ人ぞしきく
たのしき

ちぼうのきもんのしけに
けふるて一ちきかれ
樓（[illegible]）のきざいつきの[illegible]
かりしやのまこよ
ろとけのきうり
[illegible]

わるくはまく
信心者（しんじんじや）も法華者（ほつけじや）も
われが極楽（ごくらく）ぞ
いしもやいん

大日坊
文平画

2 Amida Buddha

18th century
Hanging scroll; ink and colors on paper
12 5/16 × 9 5/16 inches

Inscriptions:

HOTOKE
Tsuchi ya ki ya ishi ya kane ni te
tsukuru yori hotoke ni
tsukure hito no kokoro o

BUDDHA
Rather than making a Buddha from clay
or wood or stone or metal, mold one's heart
to that of the Buddha

TARIKI
Tanomasete tanomare tamau midanareba
tanomu kokoro mo wareto omowaji

SALVATION
Buddha lets people ask [for many things];
it is not up to us to judge those who ask

NENJU
Mimi ni kake mata wa kubi ni mo kakeru juzu
kokoro ni kakeru hito zo sukunaki

ROSARY
[Many people] hang it on their ears and necks,
but few are those who hang it on their hearts

Ōtsu-e no Mida mo kokoro no kakedokoro
kakedokorokoso ichidaiji narikere

Ōtsu pictures of Amida Buddha
should be hung on the heart;
it is the heart, not the wall,
which is important

Satsuki yama ga itsumo shimuku
orishi haru ni kore ga hotoke no
na nori keri

My heart always looks toward
Mount Satsuki in spring;
this is how Buddha shows himself

Aru hito iwaku
Shinja to naku wagasha
izure ka gokuraku e ōjō
itaruya ikan

Someone said that those who cry like me
will arrive in paradise;
what do you think?

Worship of Amida, the Buddha of Infinite Light, became prevalent in Japan during the late Heian period (794–1185). One reason for Amida's popularity was the widespread belief in *mappō*, a period of ten thousand years during which the Buddha's law would be ignored and the world would be cast into chaos and corruption. By Japanese calculation, *mappō* would commence in 1052. According to the leading evangelists of the day, during this dreaded period people would be incapable of achieving salvation without divine intercession. In eons past, Amida had vowed that, upon achieving Buddhahood, he would create a paradise where all sentient souls could strive toward enlightenment without the pain and suffering associated with life on earth. The only requirements for rebirth in Amida's paradise were a firm belief in his saving grace and recitation of his name at the moment of death. The simplicity of this belief and the promise of paradise attracted many adherents among the common people, and eventually Amida's followers became the largest Buddhist group in Japan.

One popular subject for paintings of Amida shows him descending from the heavens to receive the soul of a dying devotee. Known as *raigō*, or Welcoming Descent, these paintings vividly illustrate Amida's boundless compassion and concern for his followers. Amida is usually pictured with his attendant bodhisattvas: Seishi, whose hands are held in prayer, and Kannon, who holds a lotus throne intended for the soul of the faithful worshiper. Amida may also be accompanied by a host of heavenly musicians and divine beings, foreshadowing the celestial population of paradise.

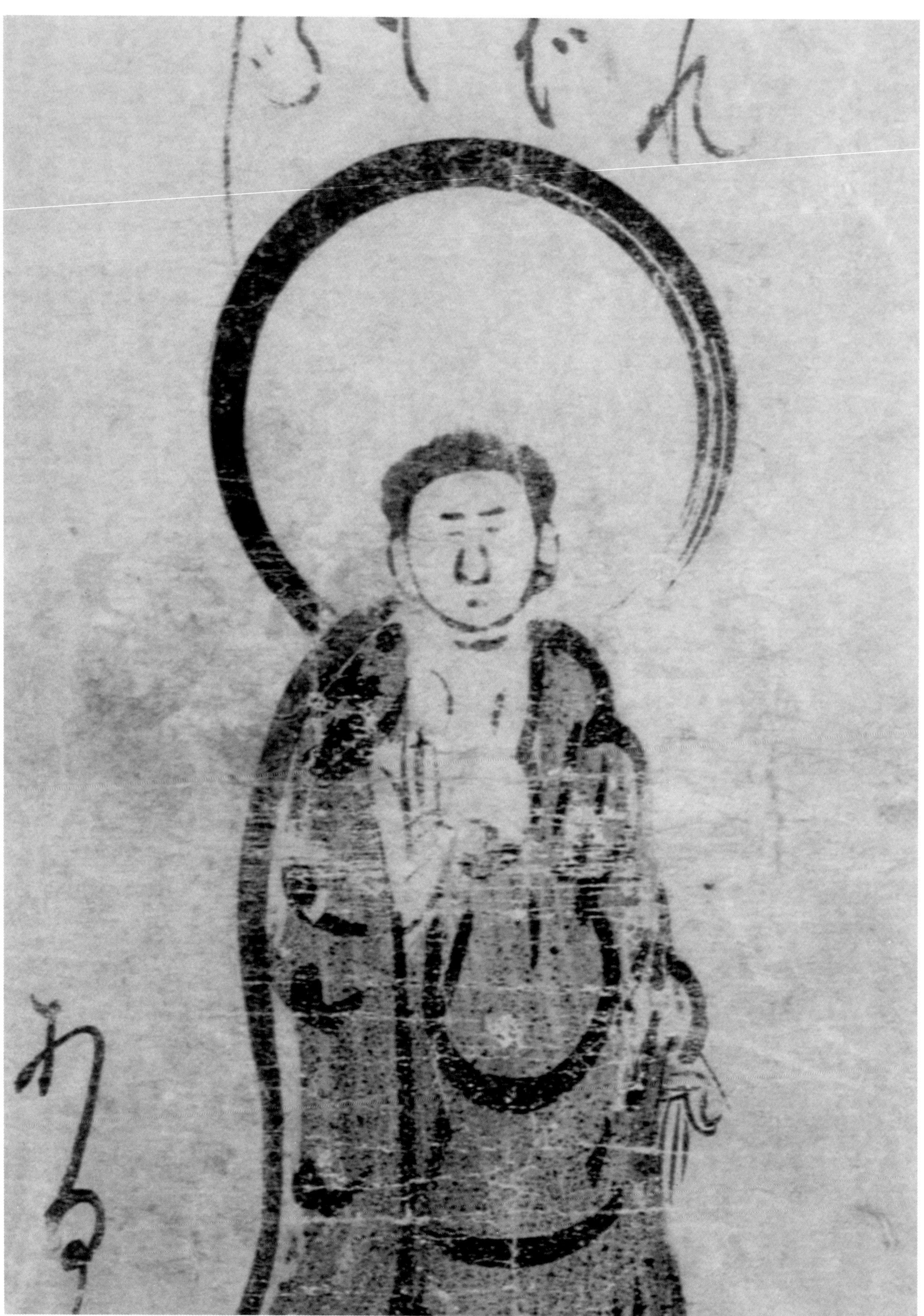

Paintings of Amida's descent were among the earliest images by Ōtsu-e artists. In this work, Amida floats downward on a cloud, now barely visible as a pale green area beneath the cushion at his feet. His hands are held in a symbolic gesture (*mudra*) of welcome. As a Buddha who has renounced worldly possessions, he wears the flowing robes of a monk, embellished by the artist with flakes of brass, now darkened by age. In keeping with iconographic precedent, his divinity is indicated by a halo, adroitly painted in a single sweeping brushstroke.

The earliest images of Amida by Ōtsu-e artists were produced in the mid-seventeenth century, but the small scale and the addition of didactic inscriptions suggest that this work dates from the last half of the eighteenth century. The signature in the lower left, which reads "painted by Matahei of Japan," is problematic. Matahei, a fictitious character in a puppet play by Chikamatsu Monzaemon (1653–1724), was a country bumpkin with a talent for painting. In the play, among many astonishing artistic feats, he is credited with creating Ōtsu-e. Over time, people confused this literary character with Iwasa Matabei (1578–1650), an artist of the Tosa school and an early proponent of the ukiyo-e style. Thus, although Ōtsu-e were the products of anonymous amateur artists, there remained some belief, based partly on fact and partly on fiction, in the shadowy figure of Matahei. Catering to this popular belief, some artists in the late eighteenth century signed Matahei on their works.

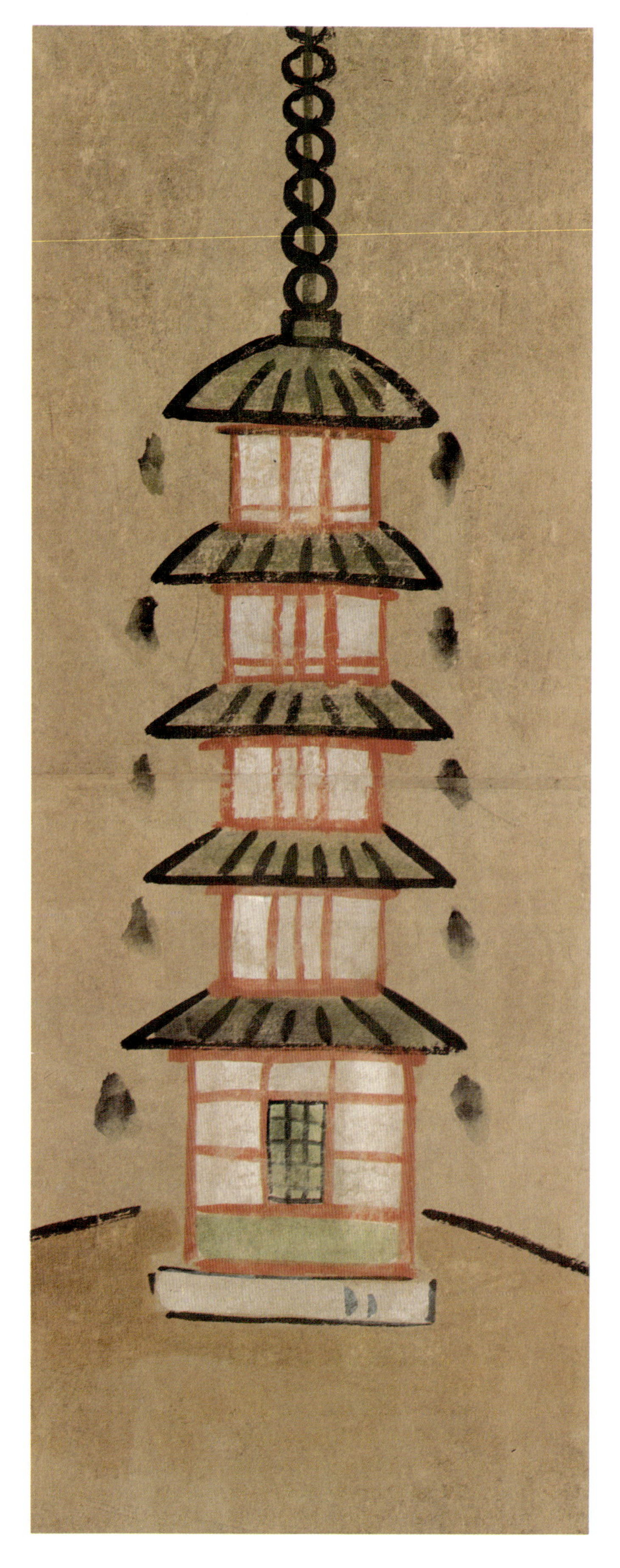

3

Pagoda (*Tō*)
18th century
Hanging scroll; ink and colors on paper
23 3/16 × 9 1/8 inches

In the earliest period of Ōtsu-e production, iconic representations of Buddhist deities predominated. Later, artists also painted images of pagodas. Of the many buildings in a Buddhist temple complex, none is more impressive than the pagoda, towering above the trees and dwarfing the neighboring edifices. Symbolically, the pagoda is the focus of great veneration. Its origins can be traced to ancient India, where hemispherical mounds of pounded earth, called *stupa*, were built to enclose relics of the historical Buddha, Sakyamuni. In China, this format developed into a multiple-roofed structure of stone or wood. The most common type of pagoda in Japan had three or five roofs and was capped by an elaborate bronze spire with nine rings. A holy relic placed within the stone foundation or beneath the central wooden pillar made the entire building a focus of worship.

Ōtsu-e artists made no attempt to render the pagoda's architectural volume or to describe its complicated and characteristic bracketing system. Instead, they recorded the essential elements: a stone base, white plaster walls, timbers painted vermilion, gray tile roofs, a tall spire of disks, and bells hanging from the corners of the eaves. Summarily conceived and simply painted, their pagodas have the same charm as children's drawings of houses.

This example, typical of Ōtsu-e imagery from the late seventeenth and early eighteenth centuries, consists of two sheets of paper joined to form a vertical format. Later renditions were done on a single sheet of paper, and the pagoda was sometimes shown as if seen from one corner. This simply and naïvely painted image possesses a monumentality not often associated with Ōtsu-e.

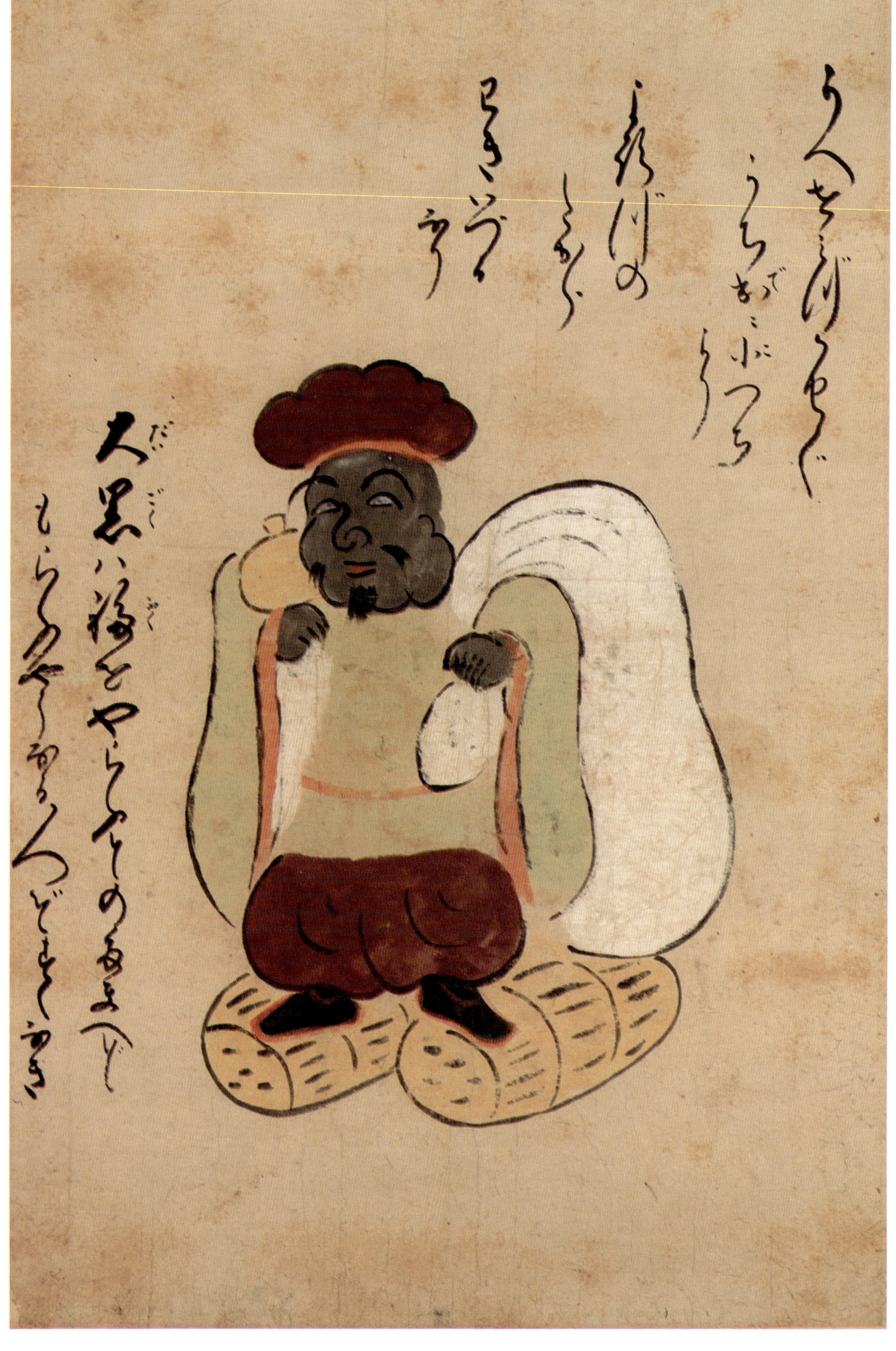

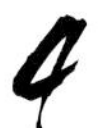

Daikoku

Late 18th century

Hanging scroll; ink and colors on paper

16⅜ × 10⅞ inches

Inscriptions:

Ue o mizu kasegu
uchide no kozuchi yori
man no takara waki izuru nari
Work diligently, and from the magic mallet
will appear ten thousand treasures

Daikoku wa fuku o yarou to notamaedo
marauyou naru hito zo sukunaki
Daikoku promises to bring us good luck,
but those who will receive it are few

Daikoku was originally an ancient Hindu deity, Mahakala, associated with darkness and fertility, and thus is usually pictured with blue or black skin. Although Daikoku appears in esoteric Buddhist imagery as a wrathful deity with three faces and six arms, a gentler, more approachable manifestation prevailed by the seventh or eighth century in China. In this form he holds a bag of gold and treasures, which in his munificence he bestows on faithful followers.

Daikoku is also one of the Seven Gods of Good Fortune (*shichi fukujin*), a group of deities of various origins that had been adopted into Japanese popular worship from China as early as the fifteenth century. Fully humanized, Daikoku wears a Chinese costume with wide sleeves, a belted jacket, baggy pants, and a large floppy hat. In Japan, the Chinese characters used to write Daikoku are the same as those denoting the native Shinto god Ōkuni. The characteristics of the two gods, never clearly defined, eventually became confused. Perhaps for this reason, Daikoku also came to be associated with agriculture and is worshiped in parts of Japan as a god of the fields. Consequently, he is usually shown standing on bales of rice, a standard measure of wealth and a symbol of good harvest. In Japanese painting, Daikoku often appears with the other gods of luck, riding in the *takarabune*, or treasure ship. Such humorously conceived images were appropriately auspicious for display at New Year's, suggesting that the coming year would bring wealth and prosperity to the entire household.

Daikoku seems to have been a favorite theme for Ōtsu-e artists, beginning in the seventeenth century, when religious subject matter predominated. In addition to this standard representation, Daikoku was irreverently shown wrestling with the god of longevity or shaving his elongated head (see cat. nos. 5 and 6) and chasing or being chased by demons.

Daikoku's felicitous nature and his dedication to accommodating humankind's materialistic desires ensured his popularity. In Ōtsu-e, the precious contents of his bag are usually suggested by a design of orange jewels, but in this example the pigment has worn away, so the bag looks unadorned. Daikoku also holds a magic mallet that produces a shower of precious jewels from whatever it strikes. The inclusion of moralizing inscriptions on this work, exhorting people to work hard without thought of reward, is characteristic of Ōtsu-e from the second half of the eighteenth century.

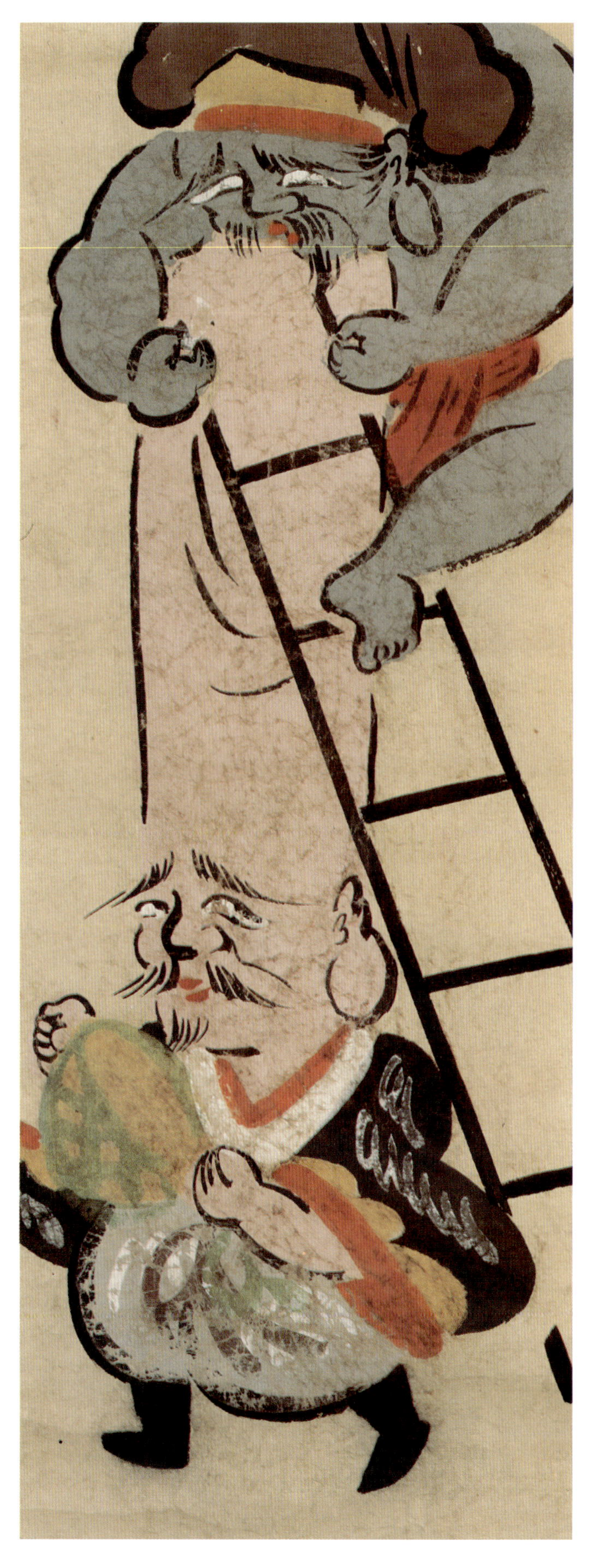

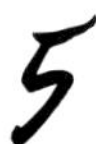

Daikoku Shaving the Head of Fukurokuju
18th century
Hanging scroll; ink and colors on paper
24 × 9$\frac{1}{16}$ inches

In preparation for undertaking the monumental task of shaving the head of Fukurokuju, the god of longevity, Daikoku has stripped down to his red loincloth. This painting shows him precariously perched on a ladder. Gripping a small razor in his right hand, he worriedly goes about his work. Fukurokuju, holding a bowl to catch the hairs as they fall, peers skeptically upward at his earnest companion.

Like Daikoku, Fukurokuju is often included among the Seven Gods of Good Fortune (*shichi fukujin*). His distinguishing feature is an extremely elongated cranium, probably meant to suggest the vast wisdom accumulated over his long life. Originating in popular folk beliefs in China, Fukurokuju became a favorite theme of ukiyo-e artists in Japan during the Edo period (1600–1868), and his long head was used for comic effect in countless images.

Ōtsu-e artists, as this painting well illustrates, also saw humorous possibilities in Fukurokuju's unusual attribute. Using bold, contrasting colors and simple, energetic black outlines, this artist designed a masterly composition by placing Daikoku at the very top, seemingly crowded off the paper by the impossible tallness of Fukurokuju's head. The painting's vivacity and the double-sheet format suggest a date in the first half of the eighteenth century. The subject remained popular, however, and was one of approximately ten Ōtsu-e themes that continued to be painted in great numbers during the nineteenth century.

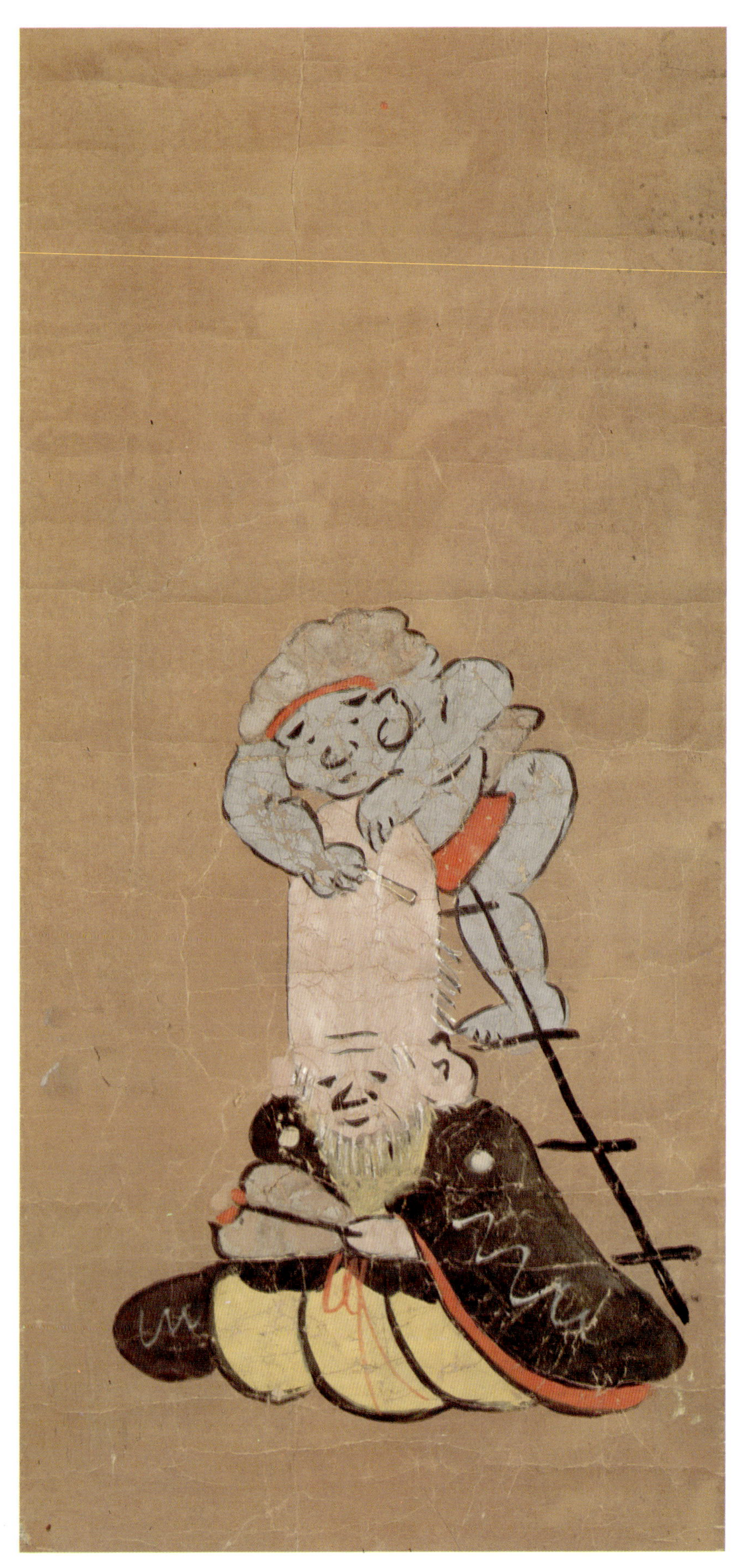

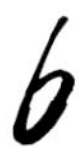

Daikoku Shaving the Head of Fukurokuju
18th century
Hanging scroll; ink and colors on paper
20¼ × 9¾ inches

The playful irreverence of Ōtsu-e artists found a receptive audience among the hedonistic population of the Edo period (1600–1868). People delighted in visual parodies, caricature, and satire. They enjoyed images of lofty deities or classical paragons caught up in worldly concerns or indulging in earthly pleasures—for example, Bodhidharma, the Indian sage credited with founding Ch'an (Zen) Buddhism in China, succumbing to the charms of a beautiful woman, or Kume, one of the Taoist Immortals, falling from the sky when distracted by the sight of a woman's bare legs. This painting suggests that even the god of longevity is vain enough of his appearance to require that his enormous head be laboriously shaved. The easy humor of such paintings ensured their popularity, and many examples remain (fig. 1).

Later ukiyo-e artists may have been influenced by early Ōtsu-e of this theme. Suzuki Harunobu (1724–70) created at least two compositions showing the god of longevity having his head shaved by a courtesan of the pleasure districts. Not only is the ancient sage narcissistic, he apparently has a proclivity for the company of beautiful young women.

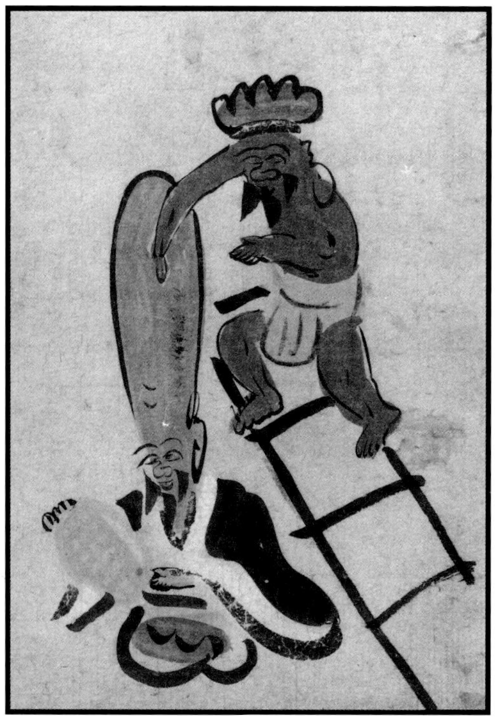

Fig. 1
Daikoku Shaving the Head of Fukurokuju
18th century
The Minneapolis Institute of Arts
Gift of an anonymous St. Paul friend

The diminutive figures and rather tentative brushwork in this painting indicate a mid- to late-eighteenth-century date. The theme remained popular into the nineteenth century, when such images were purchased as charms to ensure a long life.

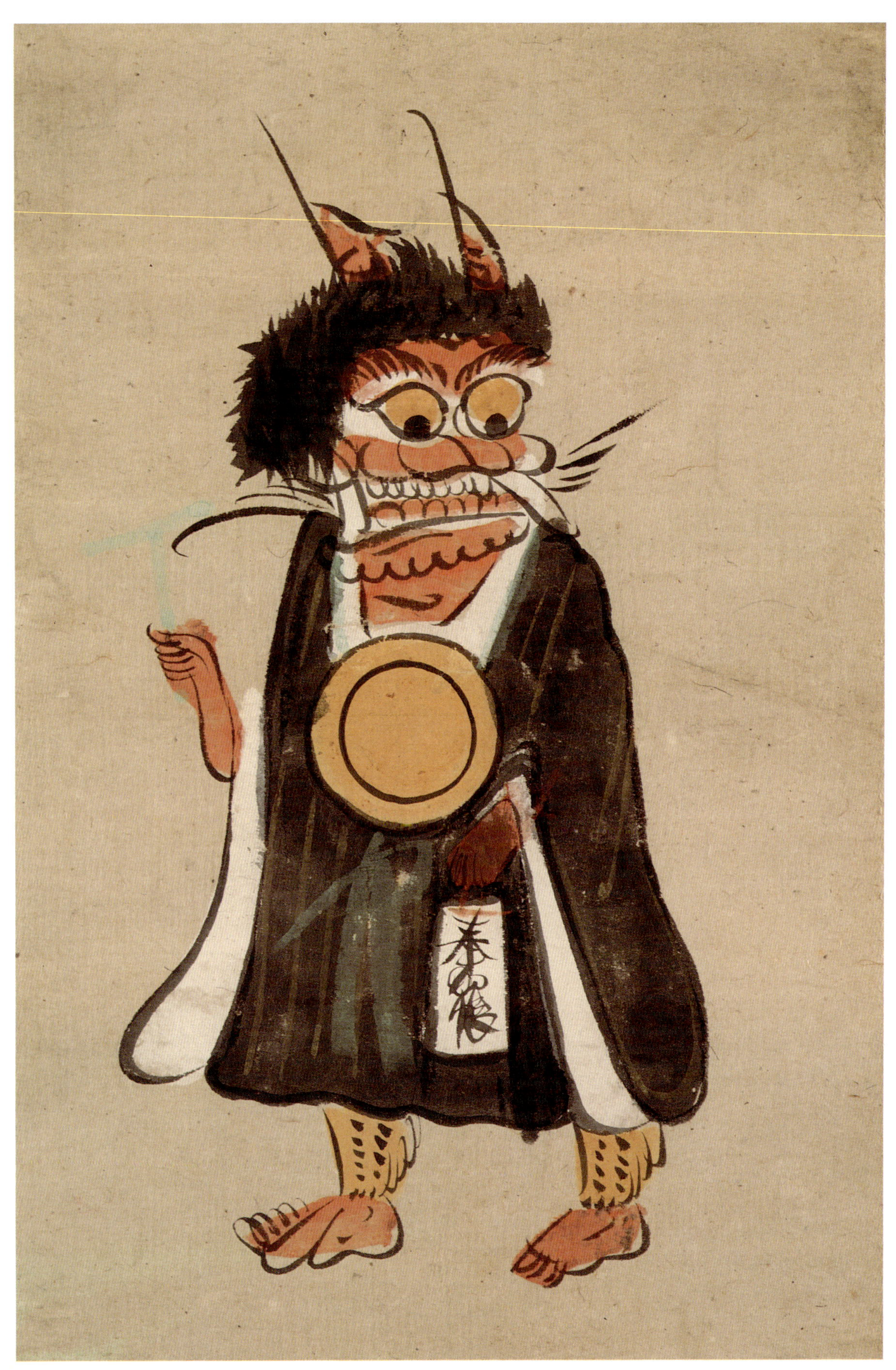
奉加帳

7 Demon Reciting Buddhist Prayers

(*Oni no nembutsu*)
18th century
Hanging scroll; ink and colors on paper
13¼ × 8⅞ inches

Oni are horned, fanged, and generally ferocious demons whose actions range from the truly sinister to the benignly humorous. They often represent forces of nature, such as wind and thunder. In Buddhism, the terrible judgments of Emma, the arbiter of hell, are carried out with sadistic glee by grotesquely muscled *oni*.

The *oni* in this painting is dressed in the black robes of a Buddhist priest. With a brass gong hung around his neck, a small hammer in his right hand, and a list of followers in his left, he chants the *nembutsu*, an invocation to Amida Buddha (see cat. no. 2) for the salvation of all souls. Japanese artists delighted in the simple humor of such unlikely juxtapositions as a demon masquerading as a priest. A favorite theme of the monk-painter Shunsō (1750–1835) was an *oni* earnestly practicing Zen meditation. Another image found among Ōtsu-e shows an *oni* climbing into a bath, as if such creatures could possibly be concerned with cleanliness. It is, in all probability, a parody of risqué ukiyo-e paintings and prints of women in various states of undress as they prepare for bathing.

Chanting *oni* may have been a satirical comment on corrupt Buddhist priests. Later images often bear moralizing poems (*dōka*) which point out that *oni* (and, by implication, evil people) show no sympathy for others while calling upon the Buddha for their own benefit. On the other hand, an *oni* reciting Buddhist prayers may suggest a repentant demon. In any case, such images were purchased during the nineteenth century as talismans to prevent infants from crying at night.[1]

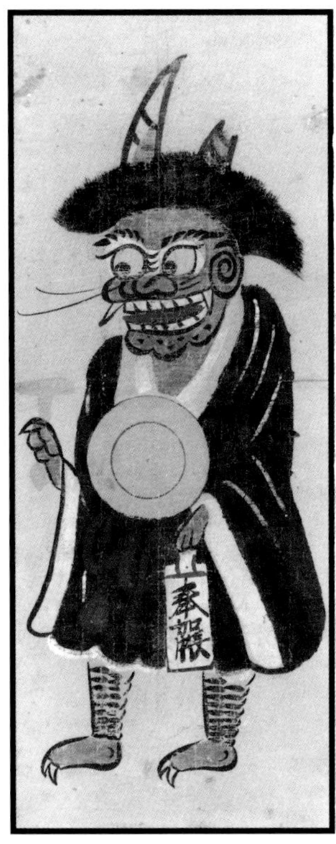

Fig. 2
Demon Reciting Buddhist Prayers
18th century
The Minneapolis Institute of Arts
Gift of Mrs. Charles B. Meech

These popular images of demons often served as signboards for shops in Ōtsu and Oiwake (see illustration, page 6). Depictions of *oni* date as early as the late seventeenth century and were produced in great quantity into the nineteenth. The appearance of the *oni* varied. Sometimes the demon has one broken horn, and sometimes he carries a folded umbrella on his back. The earliest images of *oni* seem to have adhered to traditional iconography, in which the demons have claws for fingers and two talonlike toes (fig. 2). In this eighteenth-century example, the hands and feet are distinctly human, with five fingers and toes executed in looping brushwork.

1. Ono Tadashige, "Ōtsu-e kō," in *Kaidō ni umareta minga: Ōtsu-e* (Kyoto: Korin-sha, 1991), p. 236.

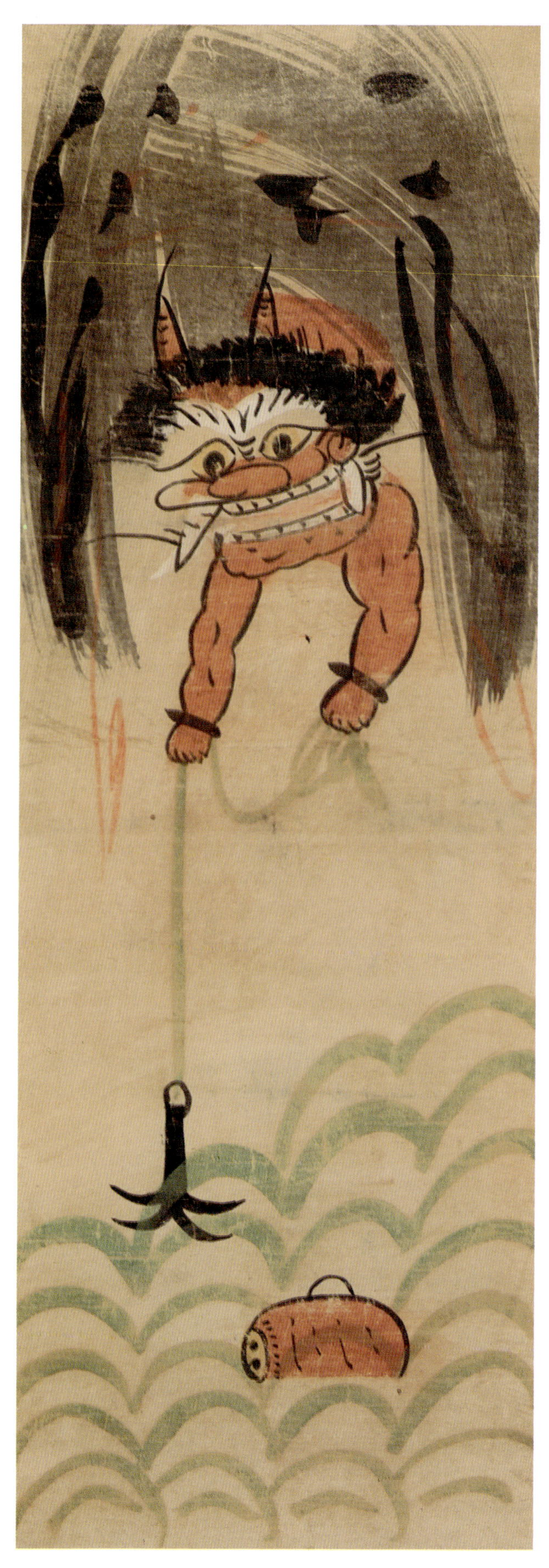

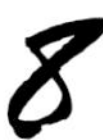

The God of Thunder and His Drum
(*Kaminari to taiko*)
18th century
Hanging scroll; ink and colors on paper
25³⁄₁₆ × 9½ inches

Personification of the natural phenomena of wind and thunder has a long history in Asia. Ultimately deriving from Indian mythology, the gods of wind and thunder became part of the Buddhist pantheon and were illustrated in wall paintings and illuminated sutras in China and Japan from an early date.[1] The wind god is generally shown holding a large bag, inflated by wind and billowing across his shoulders. The god of thunder grips two rods, which he uses to strike a series of drums revolving around him in a great circle. Both are usually depicted running atop swirling clouds, far above the world beneath them.

Rather than emphasizing the mysterious and frightening power of the god of thunder, Ōtsu-e artists humanized the deity by having him fall victim to the same misfortunes that plague ordinary people. In this painting, he has accidentally dropped his drum into the ocean. Leaning precariously out of the ominous clouds, he frantically fishes for his drum, using a heavy black hook. Meanwhile, the storm rages on, apparently without the boom and rumble associated with lightning.

The simple yet energetic technique of Ōtsu-e artists is evident in the broad rendering of the clouds; a few brushstrokes of gray accented by dabs of black denote the thunderheads. Lightning is suggested by thin, angular lines of orange surrounding the comical god. Below, the drum bobs on waves naïvely painted as a repetitious series of scalloped green lines. This artlessness, however, only contributes to the childlike immediacy and easy humor.

It is thought that this theme was first painted in the early eighteenth century. Later, when talismanic powers came to be associated with certain Ōtsu-e during the nineteenth century, images of the god of thunder were purchased and hung in homes as protection against lightning.[2]

1. See Wakisaka Atsushi, "Fujin raijin no zuzō teki keifu to Sotatsu hitsu 'Fujin raijin zu,'" *Osaka Shiritsu Bijutsukan kiyō*, 1984, no. 4:5–26.
2. Kiyoshi Yokoi, *Early Ōtsu-e* (Tokyo: Mayuyama, 1958), p. 8.

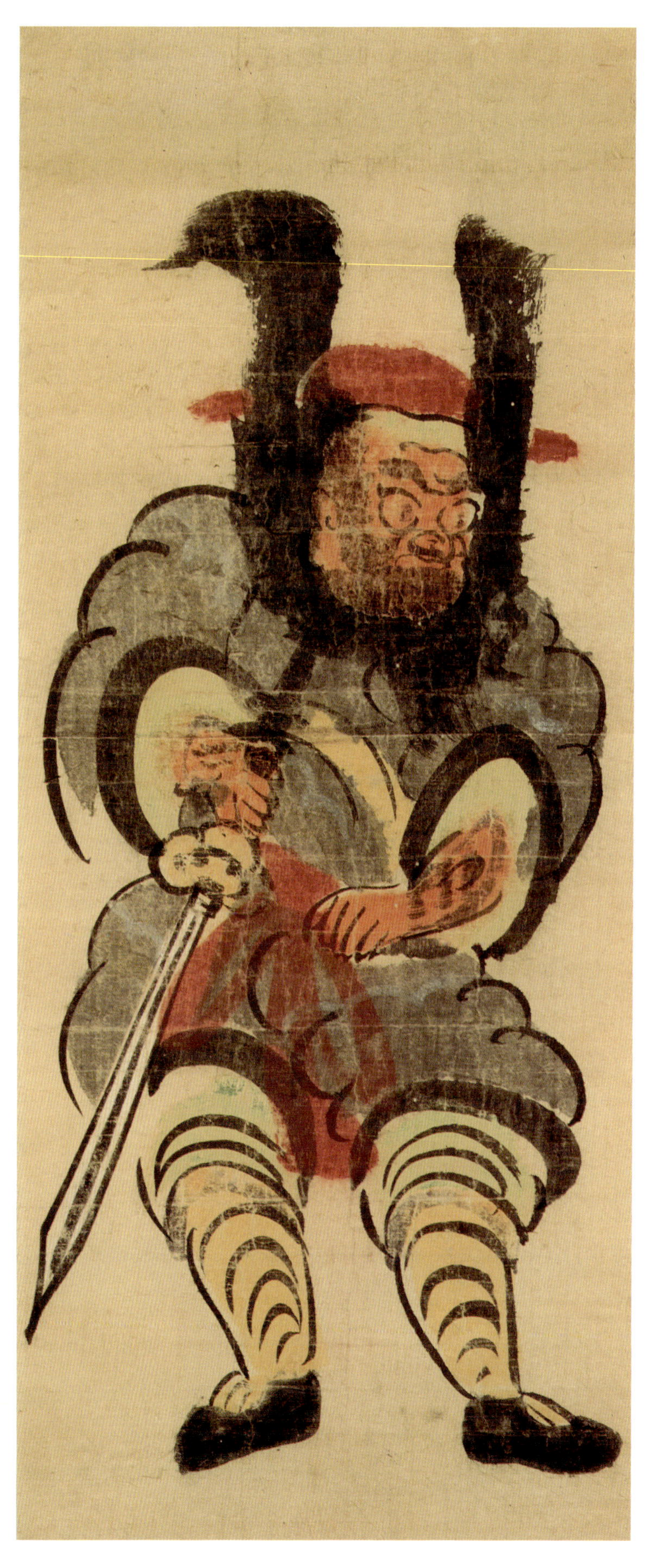

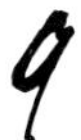

Shōki the Demon Queller
18th century
Hanging scroll; ink and colors on paper
22⁹⁄₁₆ × 9½ inches

According to legend, the Chinese emperor Ming-huang (reigned 713–756) once had a dream in which a mischievous demon entered the royal bedchamber, stole his jade flute and his favorite consort's perfume bag, and danced irreverently about the room. Just as the emperor was about to call the palace guards, a huge figure with a black, bristling beard and bulging eyes suddenly appeared, seized the demon, gouged out its eyes and proceeded to devour it. This was the spirit of Chung K'uei, a brilliant scholar who had successfully completed the imperial examinations but was denied his degree because of his repulsive appearance. In despair he committed suicide. Out of pity, the former emperor Kao-tsu granted Chung K'uei an official burial. The spirit of the scholar, touched by the emperor's kindness, vowed to free the realm of demons for all eternity.

In Japan, Shōki (Chung K'uei) was readily adopted into popular mythology. Paintings of the demon queller date as early as the Kamakura period (1185–1333) and became increasingly plentiful in the succeeding centuries. Eventually Shōki came to be associated with the ceremonies surrounding Boys' Day Festival (*tango no sekku*), held on the fifth day of the fifth month. The arrival of this date had long been anticipated with dread, because people believed that it precipitated illness and calamity, especially among boys. Various strategies were developed to avert disaster, including hanging banners painted with images of Shōki outside the homes of families with male children. Pictures painted entirely in red were believed to prevent smallpox.[1]

Paintings of Shōki occur among Ōtsu-e from the late seventeenth century onward. He is generally shown in an aggressive stance, sword drawn, and red-faced with anger, as if he had just spotted a demon. The earliest pictures usually feature Shōki with a dreadful scowl and glaring eyes, but later images are less menacing. All paintings, however, comically depict the demon queller's great beard standing on end from the intensity of his rage. In this painting the simple, lively strokes used to define Shōki's body humorously suggest his huge, bulging muscles.

1. See Matthew Welch, "Shōki the Demon Queller," in *Japanese Ghosts and Demons: Art of the Supernatural*, ed. Stephen Addiss (New York: Braziller, 1985), pp. 81–89.

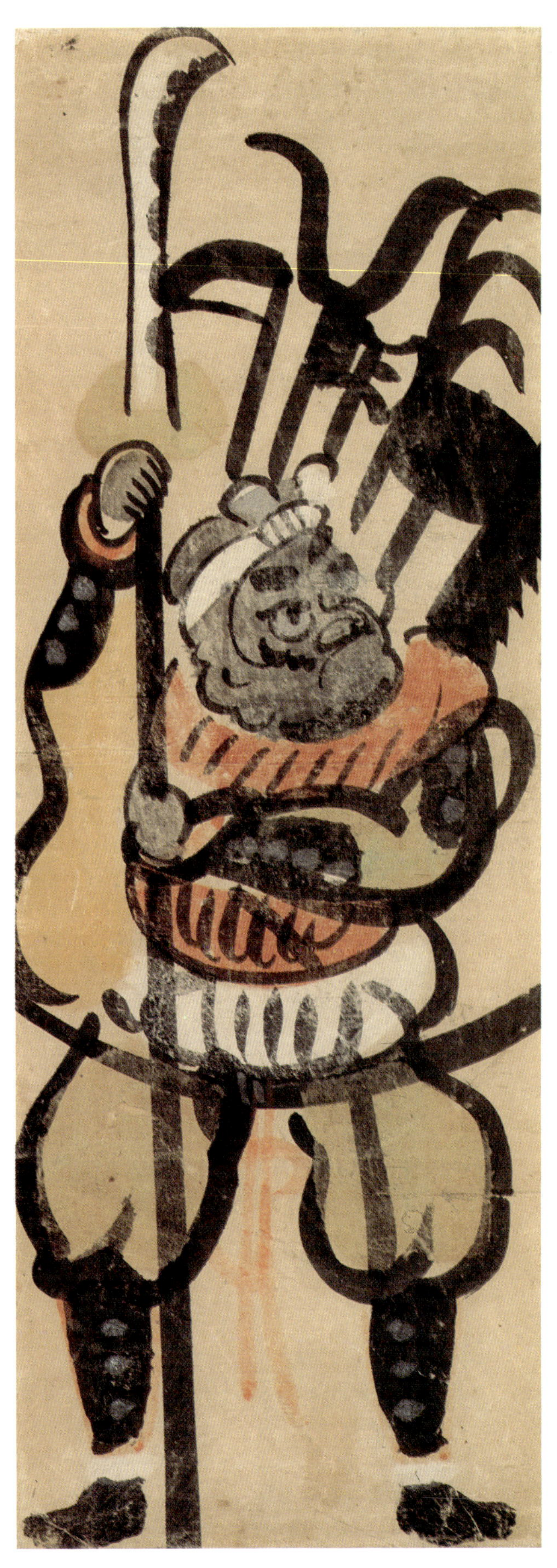

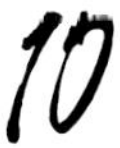

Benkei with a Halberd
(*Naginata Benkei*)
18th century
Hanging scroll; ink and colors on paper
24 3/16 × 8 13/16 inches

Benkei was a militant monk who lived during twelfth century. Proud of his physical strength and martial prowess, he vowed to collect 1,000 swords by challenging travelers crossing the Gojō Bridge in Kyoto. After successfully taking 999 swords, he encountered an elegant young man whom he almost mistook for a woman. To his surprise, the boy accepted his challenge and easily defeated him, whereupon Benkei swore to devote his life to serving the remarkable youth.

The aristocratic boy was, in fact, Yoshitsune, son of the nobleman Minamoto Yoshitomo, who was defeated in the Heiji war of 1159 by Taira Kiyomori. Although ruthless, Kiyomori had spared Yoshitomo's sons, Yoritomo and Yoshitsune. Yoshitsune was raised by monks at Kurama temple, northeast of Kyoto. According to legend, he had natural skill in martial arts and was secretly trained by the magical mountain goblins (*tengu*) who inhabited the forests near the temple.

Legends abound concerning the military exploits of Yoshitsune and his faithful retainer Benkei, and many of these provided the inspiration for Nō and Kabuki plays. The story that gives the greatest insight into the depths of Benkei's devotion to Yoshitsune is the subject of this Ōtsu-e. After Yoshitsune had waged a successful military campaign against the Taira clan, his jealous brother Yoritomo turned against him and sent an army to execute him. After several narrow escapes, Yoshitsune and Benkei were finally surrounded at Koromogawa. To give Yoshitsune time to commit an honorable suicide, Benkei single-handedly held the advancing troops at bay. Because of Benkei's fierce determination to guard his master, his body maintained its threatening posture even after he was mortally wounded.

This Ōtsu-e depicts Benkei in the moments after his death, still firmly grasping his deadly halberd, his feet planted in a resolute stance. Six additional weapons, strapped to his back, radiate outward behind him. Encircling his head is a *hachimaki*, a headband worn when great concentration is needed. His mouth is set downward in a scowl, and his eyes look defiantly upward. The bold, black brushwork strikingly conveys the warrior's masculine might. Nevertheless, the naïveté of the drawing and the gentle caricature of Benkei's face make this less a gruesome apparition than an endearing portrait of the beloved national hero.

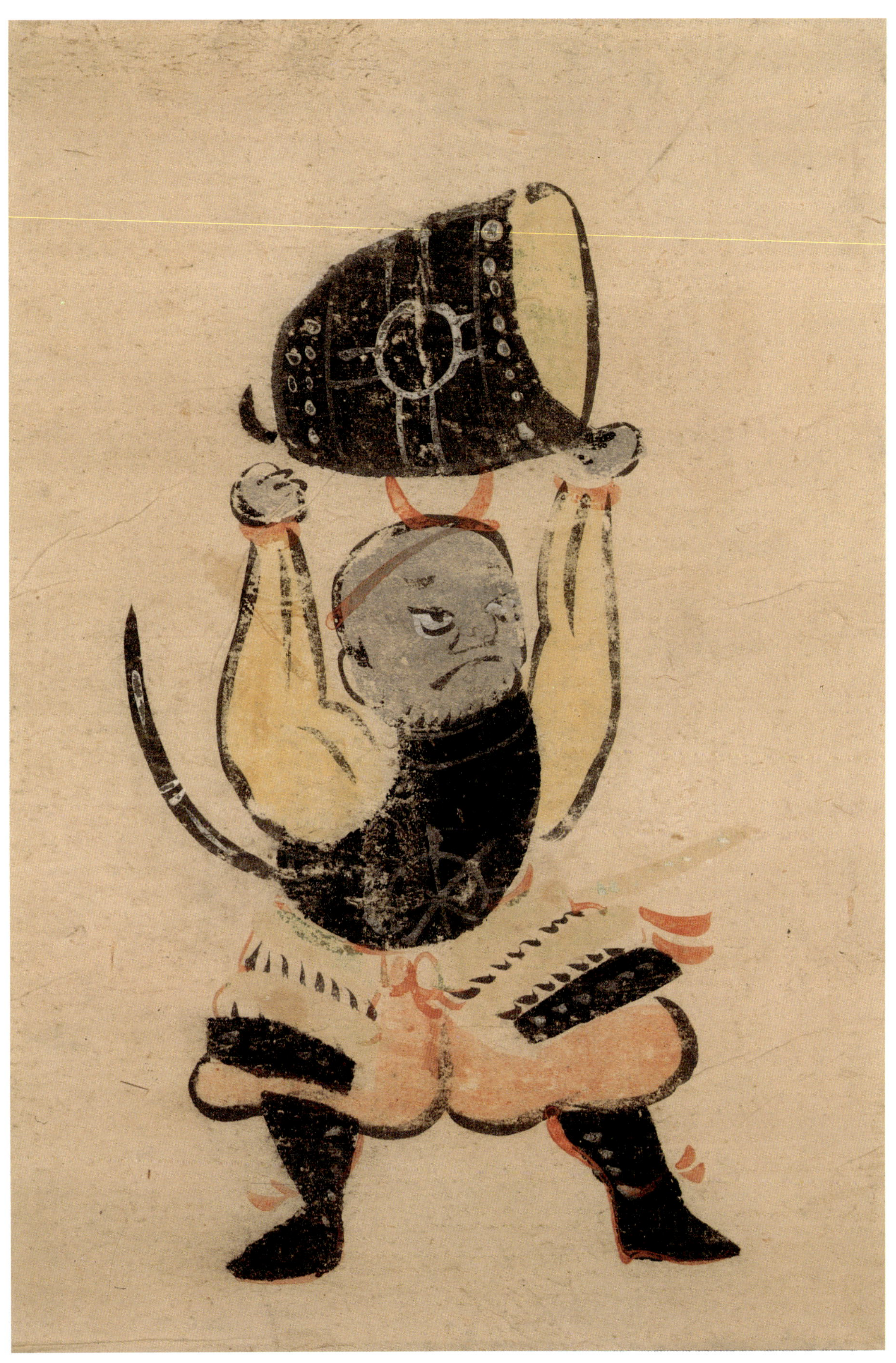

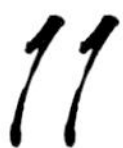

Benkei with the Temple Bell
(*Tsurigane Benkei*)
18th century
Hanging scroll; ink and colors on paper
13⅜ × 9⅛ inches

The temple bell of Miidera, said to be one of the three most prized bells in Japan, is renowned for its beautiful resonance. According to legend, when warfare broke out between the neighboring temples of Miidera and Enryakuji in the twelfth century, the warrior monk Benkei stole this bell and singlehandedly dragged it up the steep slope of Mount Hiei. Arriving at his temple home, Benkei discovered that the bell would not sound when struck. Instead, it seemed to be softly weeping. Disgusted, Benkei lifted the great bell over his head and threw it into the valley below. Crashing downward through the forest, it came to rest at the gate of Miidera.

This painting shows Benkei throwing the bell down the mountain. The relative smallness of the bell is probably meant to indicate Benkei's legendary stature. In some Ōtsu-e, Benkei holds the heavy bell aloft with only one arm, another sign of his enormous strength. Although he has a monk's shaved head, Benkei wears a sword, a black breastplate, and flaps of armor on his thighs, illustrating his militaristic tendencies. He also wears a *hachimaki*, a headband customarily worn by the Japanese when tackling a difficult task.

Benkei and the temple bell is a subject not often encountered in other schools of Japanese painting. It may have become a popular theme among Ōtsu-e artists because of Miidera temple's proximity to Ōtsu. The earliest images date from the first half of the eighteenth century; however, the diminished scale and grandeur of the figure and smaller format suggest a later date for this painting. The childlike quality of the great warrior, in spite of his firm stance and angry grimace, makes this work comically charming.

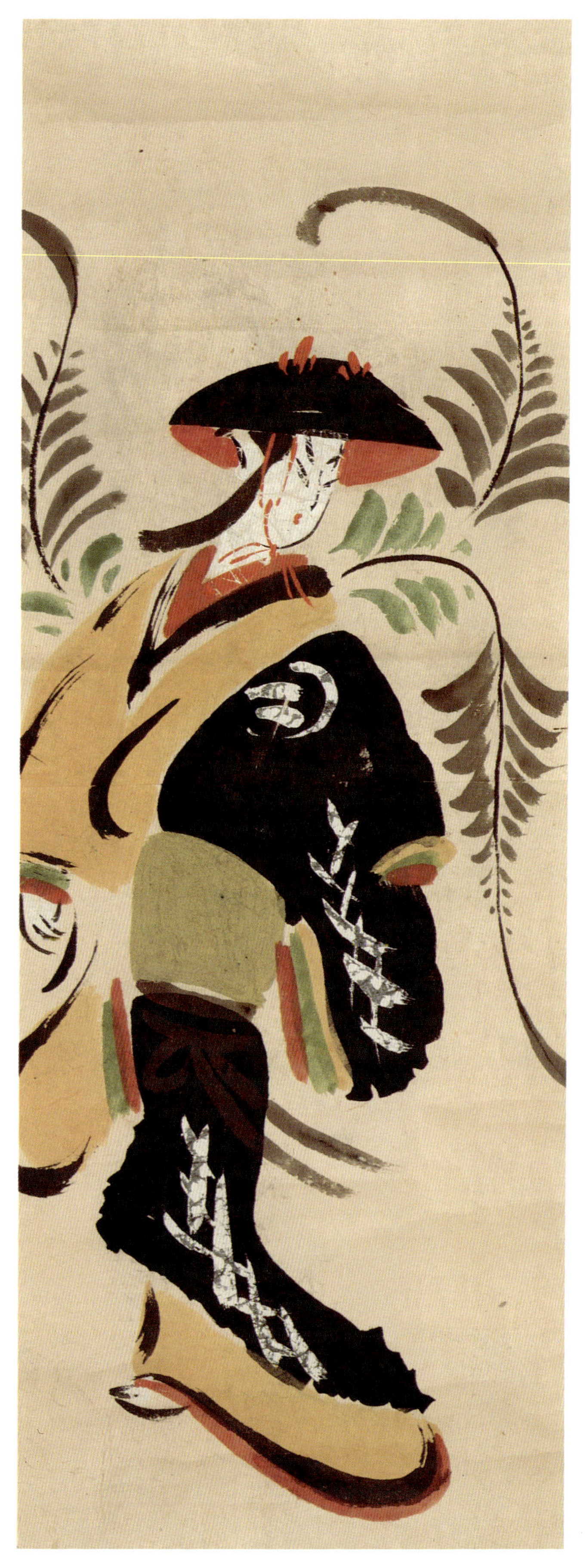

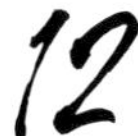

Wisteria Maiden (*Fuji musume*)
18th century
Hanging scroll; ink and colors on paper
25⅛ × 9⅜ inches

Paintings of the so-called wisteria maiden were among the most popular, and therefore most frequently produced, of all Ōtsu-e. The precise origin of this theme is obscure. Wisteria blooms in the spring, sending forth long, drooping clusters of bluish purple flowers. Excursions to view these graceful blossoms were the focus of annual viewing festivals. Perhaps the earliest images of the wisteria maiden arose from local dances performed in celebration of spring. On the other hand, the famous playwright Chikamatsu Monzaemon (1653–1724) in his play *Keisei hangonkō*, written for the puppet theater, mentions a certain lady Oyama carrying a branch of flowering wisteria across her shoulder.[1] Whether this brief passage prompted Ōtsu-e artists to create an image of the maiden or whether another source, now lost, inspired both Chikamatsu and the Ōtsu-e painters is not known. Certainly ukiyo-e artists' popular depictions of young urban beauties influenced the development of such secular themes in Ōtsu-e.

The earliest images of the wisteria maiden may date to the Genroku era (1688–1704), a period that epitomized the renaissance of plebeian culture in the bustling cities of Edo, Kyoto, and Osaka. While ukiyo-e may have influenced early wisteria maiden paintings, the subsequent popularity of this Ōtsu-e theme was certainly the inspiration for a new dance performance held at the Nakamura-za Kabuki theater in 1826, called "Fuji musume."[2]

The consistent pose of the wisteria maiden clearly derives from ukiyo-e imagery of a young woman in the very animated posture of walking one direction while looking back coquettishly over her shoulder. Unlike ukiyo-e artists, who depicted the patterns of women's robes in meticulous detail, Ōtsu-e painters indicated fabric design with a few sweeping brushstrokes of contrasting color. In this case, simple white patterns adorn the wisteria maiden's black outer kimono; rich orange, ocher, and green suggest the layers of her robe; and a broad area of olive indicates her wide obi, or sash. One of the liveliest expressions of the Ōtsu-e painting style is seen in the sprays of wisteria. Early images show the maiden holding a rather naturalistic branch of blossoms; later images, such as this, feature abstract arabesques that rhythmically swing to and fro.[3]

In the nineteenth century, when specific talismanic powers came to be associated with many of the themes of Ōtsu-e, images of the wisteria maiden were purchased in hopes of finding a good mate or to ensure the safe delivery of a baby.[4]

1. Suehiro Sachiyo, in *Kaidō ni umareta minga: Ōtsu-e* (Kyoto: Korin-sha, 1991), p. 91.
2. Kobayashi Tadashi, *Ōtsu-e* (Machida: Machida Municipal Museum, 1990), p. 54.
3. Suehiro, p. 90.
4. Ibid.

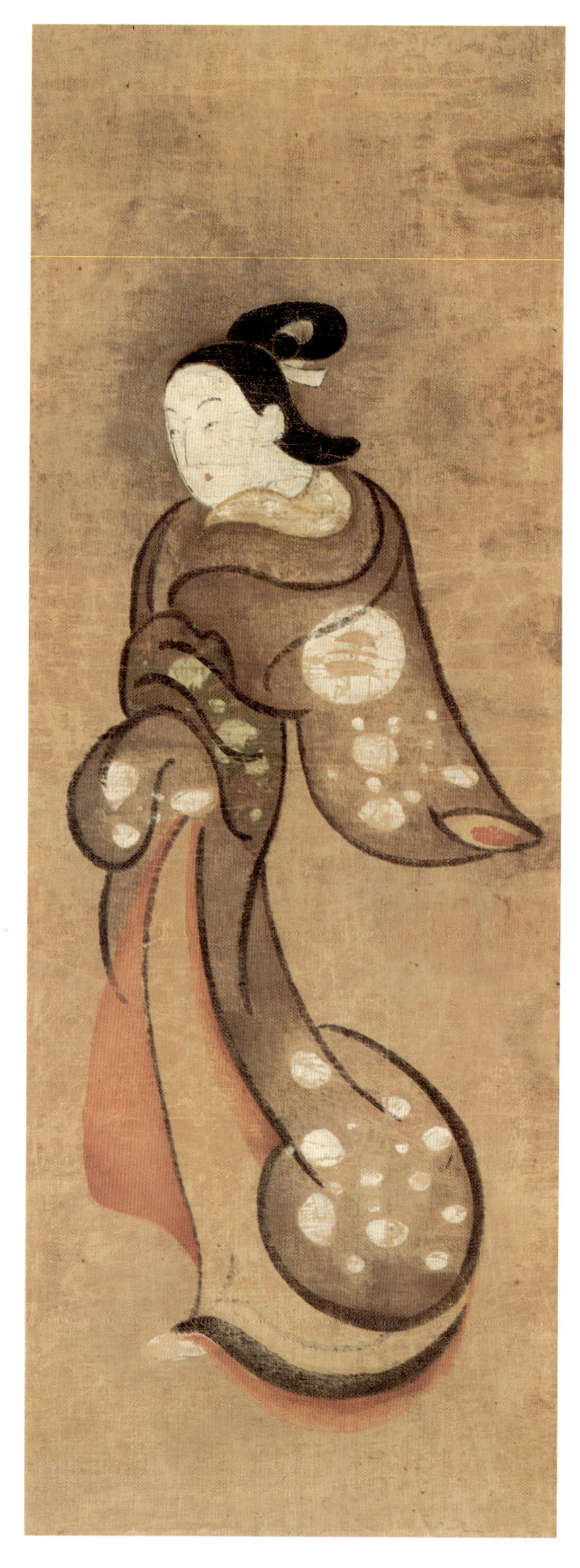

13

Courtesan (*Tayū*)
18th century
Hanging scroll; ink and colors on paper
25¼ × 9 inches

Delicately lifting her hem, this graceful beauty strides forward, her sumptuous kimono parting to reveal the red and white layers of her inner robes. She has carefully readied herself, perhaps for a romantic interlude, by powdering her skin and accentuating her tiny mouth with the brilliant red of safflower.

As Japan gradually recovered from the warfare of the fifteenth century, there emerged an interest in the peaceful pastimes and customs of an urban society. Great decorative screens were painted illustrating townspeople and idle samurai engaged in seasonal festivals, picnics, and sporting events. By the early seventeenth century, some artists began to focus on life in the licensed pleasure quarters of Edo, Kyoto, and Osaka. Known as ukiyo-e, or pictures of the floating world, these woodblock prints and paintings immortalized the women of the entertainment districts, renowned for their beauty, sophistication, and style. People clamored to purchase images of their favorite courtesans. So popular were these images, and so prolific the artists, that ukiyo-e became a major artistic trend of the Edo period (1600–1868).

Ōtsu-e artists were undoubtedly influenced by the growing interest in ukiyo-e. By the first decades of the eighteenth century, in fact, such secular themes had superseded the religious subjects of early Ōtsu-e. Borrowing poses already popular in ukiyo-e, Ōtsu-e artists rendered their subjects in sweeping outlines and bold colors. Fabric patterns, meticulously delineated by ukiyo-e artists, were abbreviated to simple yet striking designs. In this case, the artist decorated the woman's robe by scattering dots of white pigment about the hem, sleeve, and belt. Although the paper has darkened with age, the bright orange of the inner robes and the vivid green of the belt still contrast dramatically with the overall mauve of the courtesan's kimono.

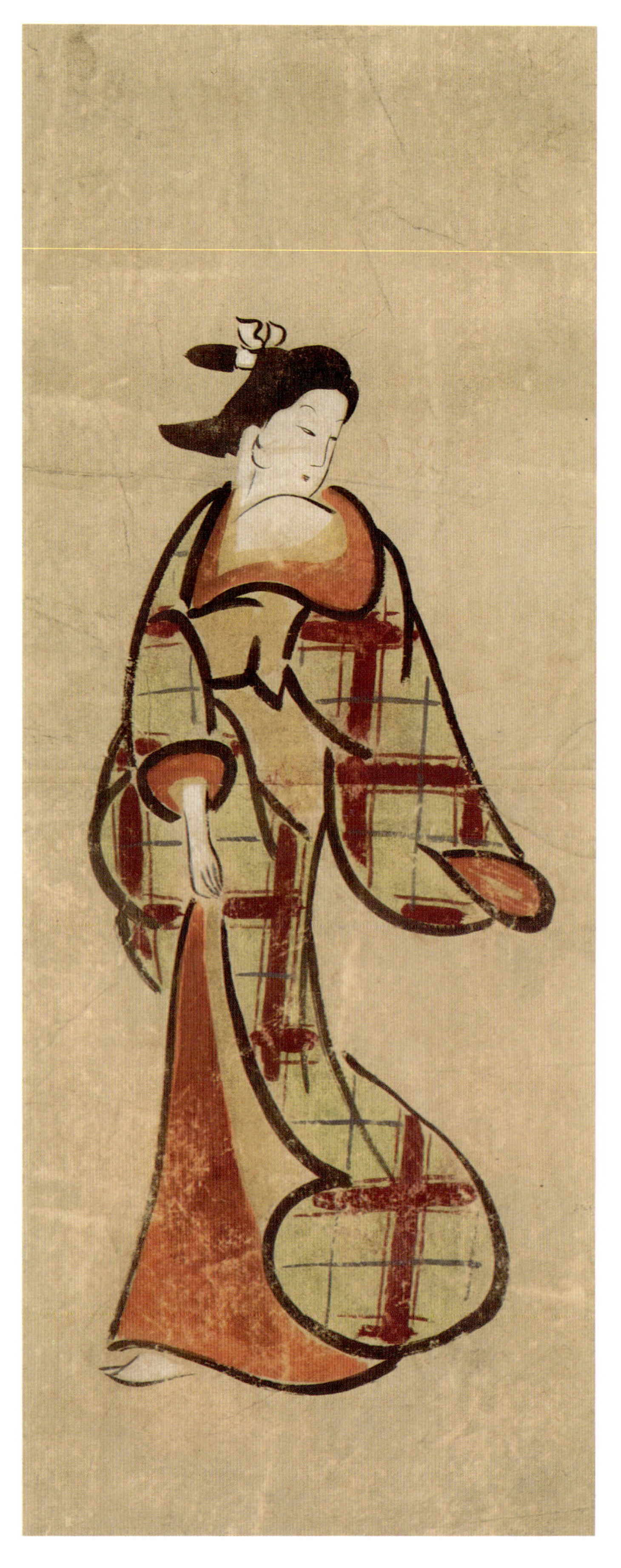

Courtesan (*Tayū*)
Late 18th or early 19th century
Hanging scroll; ink and colors on paper
23 3/16 × 9 1/8 inches

By the Kambun era (1661–73) anonymous genre painters had evolved a standardized format for depicting the beautiful women of the entertainment districts. A single figure dominated the painting surface, allowing artists to describe the gorgeous silk robes in meticulous detail, and a variety of arresting poses suggested the languid movements of the women. Especially popular was the *migaeri*, or "looking back," posture, in which the woman appears to be walking one direction and looking back over her shoulder, perhaps bidding a lover farewell with one final glance.

The Kambun style of beauty remained popular until the late seventeenth century, and this was most likely the type of painting emulated by Ōtsu-e artists when they began to use secular imagery. This painting shows a woman in the classic *migaeri* pose. Her sumptuous robes, seemingly too large for her delicate frame, have slipped off her shoulder, suggestively revealing bare skin.

While later ukiyo-e artists went on to develop elaborate compositions that included multiple figures in countless poses and articulated background scenery, Ōtsu-e artists seem to have remained content with the simple Kambun beauty style. Similarly, Ōtsu-e beauties consistently exhibit the simple hairstyles prevalent at the turn of the eighteenth century, regardless of when they were painted, whereas ukiyo-e artists recorded the latest changes in fashion. Clearly Ōtsu-e artists were not trying to compete with metropolitan ukiyo-e painters. Rather, they produced works of naïve, even old-fashioned, charm. They specialized in a few standard renditions which they continued to paint with verve throughout the eighteenth century and into the nineteenth.

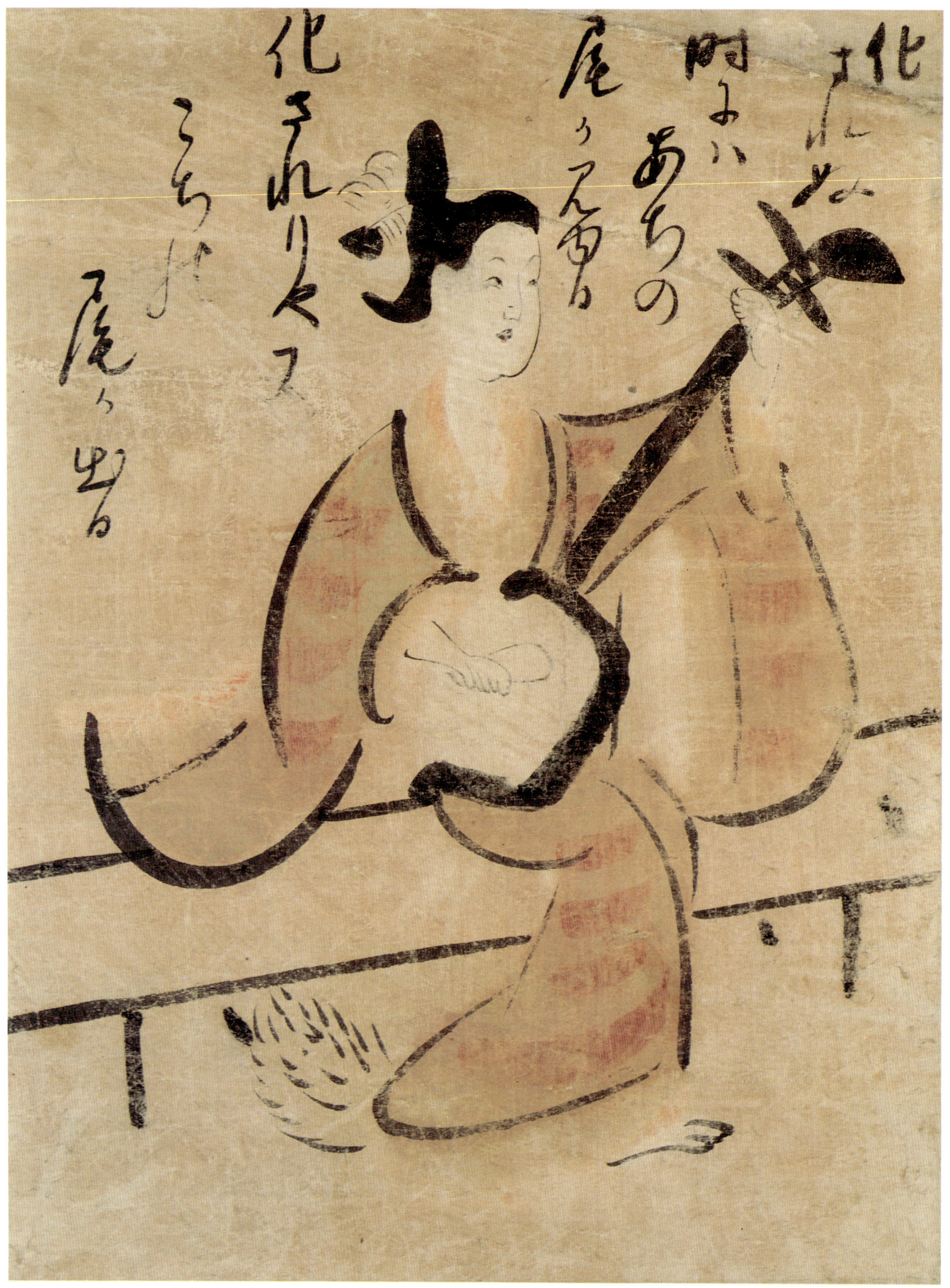

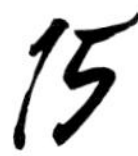

Fox Woman (*Kitsune onna*)
18th century
Hanging scroll; ink and colors on paper
11 15/16 × 9 1/8 inches

Inscription:

Bakasarenu toki ni wa
achi no o ga miyuru,
bakasarerya
mata kochi no o ga deru
When you are not deceived,
you will see her tail;
when you are deceived,
you will reveal your own tail

In Japanese folklore, foxes (*kitsune*) transform themselves into humans in order to play tricks on or otherwise beguile unsuspecting people. Though most of their mischief is innocuous, they are capable of harmful, even fatal deceptions. Foxes commonly take the shape of a beautiful woman who easily leads lovelorn men astray. Emperor Toba (reigned 1107–23), for example, is said to have been obsessively enamored of one of his concubines. Becoming progressively weaker, he fell dangerously ill. A court physician, suspecting the woman to be a malicious fox, arranged a Buddhist ceremony at which she would be obligated to offer prayers for her ailing lord. Facing an image of the Buddha, she could not maintain her deceptive guise. Before the startled eyes of the other courtiers, she changed back into a fox and fled the palace. With the malevolent fox gone, the emperor quickly recovered his health.[1]

This Ōtsu-e pictures a typical beauty of the mid-Edo period (1600–1868). Dressed in a beautiful kimono, her skin whitened by cosmetics, she is playing a three-stringed *shamisen* (a zither associated with ribald entertainment). She appears to be a woman of the licensed pleasure quarters. Protruding from the hem of her robe, however, is a bushy tail, betraying her true nature.

The inscription on this painting is less a warning about real or imagined foxes masquerading as beautiful women than a playful comment on the nature of human deceit. If you are sharp witted, it seems to imply, you will detect an insincere woman's artful pretense; if she is more cunning, she will discover your own duplicity. In short, we are all like foxes, ignobly scheming for personal gain.

Fox women do not seem to have entered Ōtsu-e artists' repertoire until the early eighteenth century. As in this painting, they are always shown seated on a low bench, playing a *shamisen*. The smaller, single-sheet format and the moralizing inscription suggest a mid- to late-eighteenth-century date for this work.

1. T. Volker, *The Animal in Far Eastern Art* (Leiden: E. J. Brill, 1975), p. 81.

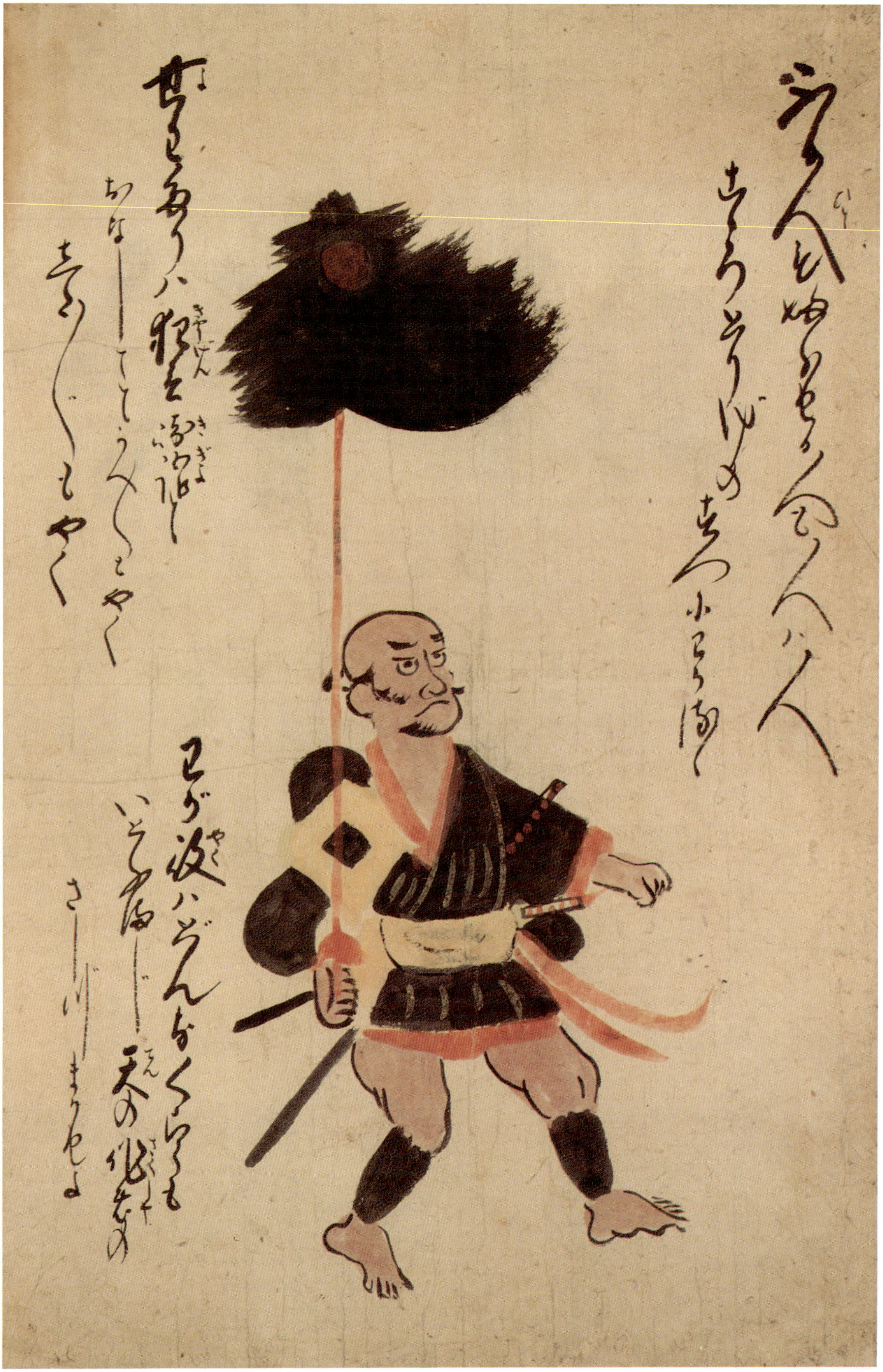

ふ人とめでたく人ハ人
きうそうじめきへ小兵衛

世の中ハ野干ぞ源なし
おなしことうくくとやく
きりしくもやく

王が役ハぞんなくらひても
いそ路じ天の作花の
さじまりもよ

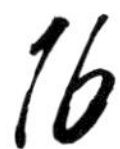

Spear Bearer (*Yarimochi yakko*)
18th century
Hanging scroll; ink and colors on paper
16⅞ × 10¹⁵⁄₁₆ inches

Inscriptions:

Furuhito mo furaseruhito mo hito wa hito
shiro tori kokoro no mizu ni wakaruru

Both those who throw spears
and those who let them, are human;
water divides those who live in a castle
and those who do not

Yowatari wa kyogen kigo to onaji koto
ue ue mo yaku shita shita mo yaku

Passing through life
is just like the flowery language of a play;
one with superior rank takes one role,
and one in an inferior position takes another

Wagayaku wa donna kurōmo itou maji
ten no sakusha no sashizu makase ni

Without concern for the hardships of my role
I will perform
as the divine playwright indicates

During the Edo period (1600–1868), the supreme military ruler of Japan (shogun) required that his provincial lords (daimyo) spend alternate years in attendance at court in Edo (present-day Tokyo). A daimyo's journey from his domain was an opportunity for a display of prestige and power. Comprising footmen, mounted warriors, high-ranking advisers, bannermen, and a variety of servants and porters, a daimyo's entourage could number in the thousands, filling the roadway for miles. Foremost in this grand procession came the spear bearers, who commanded people to prostrate themselves before the coming of the exalted lord. As they jogged jauntily along, the great tufts of furs or feathers that sheathed the long blades bounced and swung to the rhythm of their gait.

These processions were a familiar sight to residents of Ōtsu, a small town along the Tōkaidō roadway, which linked Edo and Kyoto. It is therefore not surprising that Ōtsu-e artists began to portray members of the daimyo retinue. Besides spear bearers, they depicted porters shouldering boxes, young samurai traveling by foot or on horseback, and falconers (see cat. nos. 17 and 18).

As this painting illustrates, Ōtsu-e artists represented the spear bearer as a stout man with strong legs and bare feet, clearly indicating his position as a runner in the retinue. His short black jacket is belted and hiked high, allowing him to stride forward freely. Befitting his rank as a samurai, he wears two swords. His most distinguishing characteristic, however, is the great black pom-pom of his spear. Executed with a few quick, rough brushstrokes, it enlivens the entire composition.

Ōtsu-e artists most likely began painting the spear bearer out of admiration for his impressive strength and enviable position. Some scholars suggest, however, that later images parody low-born individuals who ape their superiors' power and authority.[1] In any case, the spear bearer was among the earliest secular subjects treated by Ōtsu-e artists, and many paintings survive. During the nineteenth century, when Ōtsu-e were purchased as talismans, it was believed that images of the spear bearer helped protect travelers from harm.[2]

1. Kobayashi Tadashi, *Ōtsu-e* (Machida: Machida Municipal Museum, 1990), p. 52.
2. Kiyoshi Yokoi, *Early Ōtsu-e* (Tokyo: Mayuyama, 1958), p. 8.

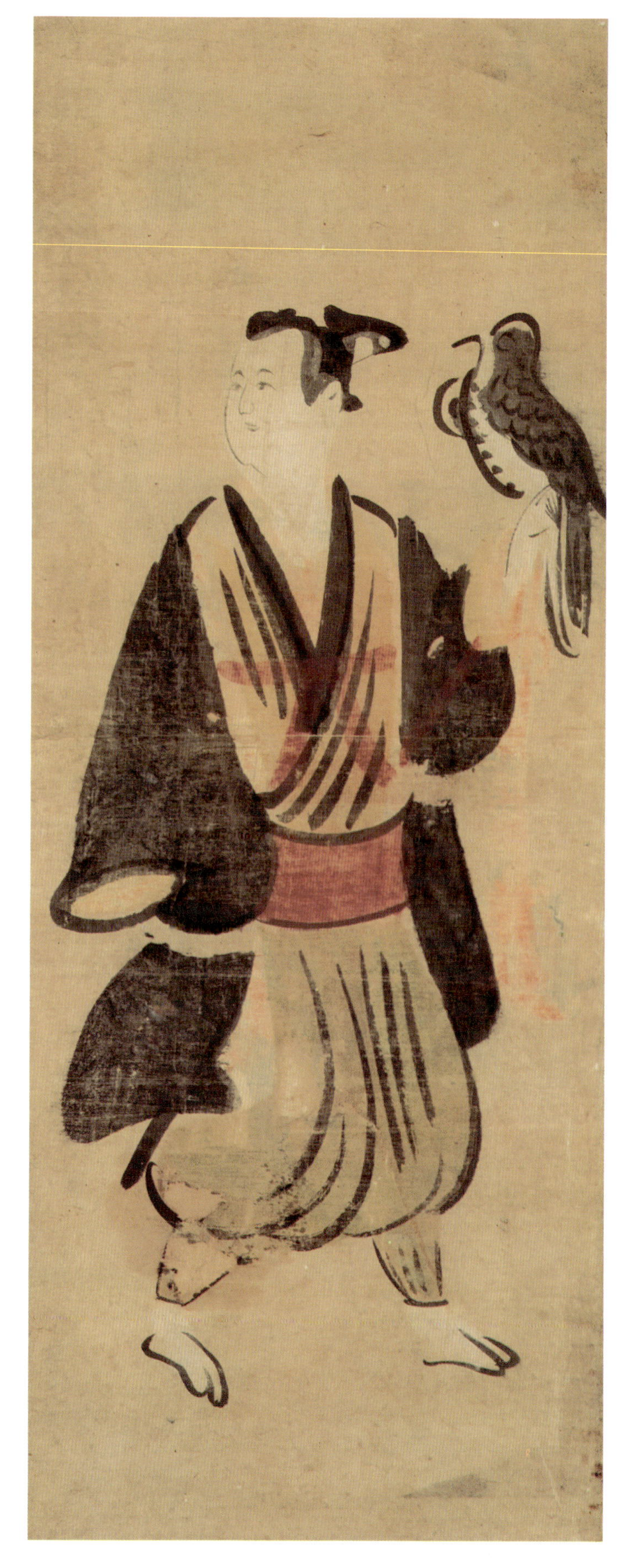

17

Falconer (*Takajō*)
18th century
Hanging scroll; ink and colors on paper
24½ × 9½ inches

The training of predatory birds for hunting and sport has a long tradition in Japan. The *Kojiki* (the earliest written history of Japan, datable to 712) records that hawking for pheasants was conducted as early as the time of Emperor Nintoku (about 319–399). Clay figures (*haniwa*) placed on top of burial mounds during the Tumulus period (about 300–710) include images of falconers with birds perched on their arms. As in many other countries, falconry was a noble pastime of the aristocracy and high-ranking warriors, and the ability to handle birds was an admired skill. During the Edo period (1600–1868), master falconers (*takajō*) were accorded special rank within the samurai hierarchy.

Although the majority of Ōtsu-e represent popular gods and legendary heroes, many subjects reflect contemporary life. Among them are at least four personages from the retinues of feudal lords (daimyo) traveling to and from Edo (Tokyo) on the Tōkaidō roadway: the spear bearer (cat. no. 16), the porter, the handsome retainer, and the falconer. Of the hundreds of men who made up a daimyo's entourage, these four in particular seem to have captured the interest of artists. Because of his exotic profession, evident from the majestic bird held high on his arm, the falconer understandably attracted great attention, and he was among the first secular subjects painted by Ōtsu-e artists during the late seventeenth and early eighteenth centuries.

Representations of falconers in Ōtsu-e are invariably idealistic, suggesting the public's romantic conception of this profession. The falconer consistently appears as a handsome young man dressed in a ceremonial jacket (*haori*), trousers (*hakama*), leggings, and formal white socks (*tabi*) and wearing his carefully groomed hair in a topknot. A vigorous youth, he is shown in action, usually striding to the right while looking to the left.

The earliest Ōtsu-e of the falconer, of which this painting is a rare example, possess a certain masculinity often lacking in later works (see cat. no. 18). He wears his clothing with casual ease. His kimono gaps open, exposing his chest, and his belt rides low on his hips; his *haori* slips loosely off his broad shoulders. This idealized image reflected the prevailing taste in masculine style at the turn of the eighteenth century.

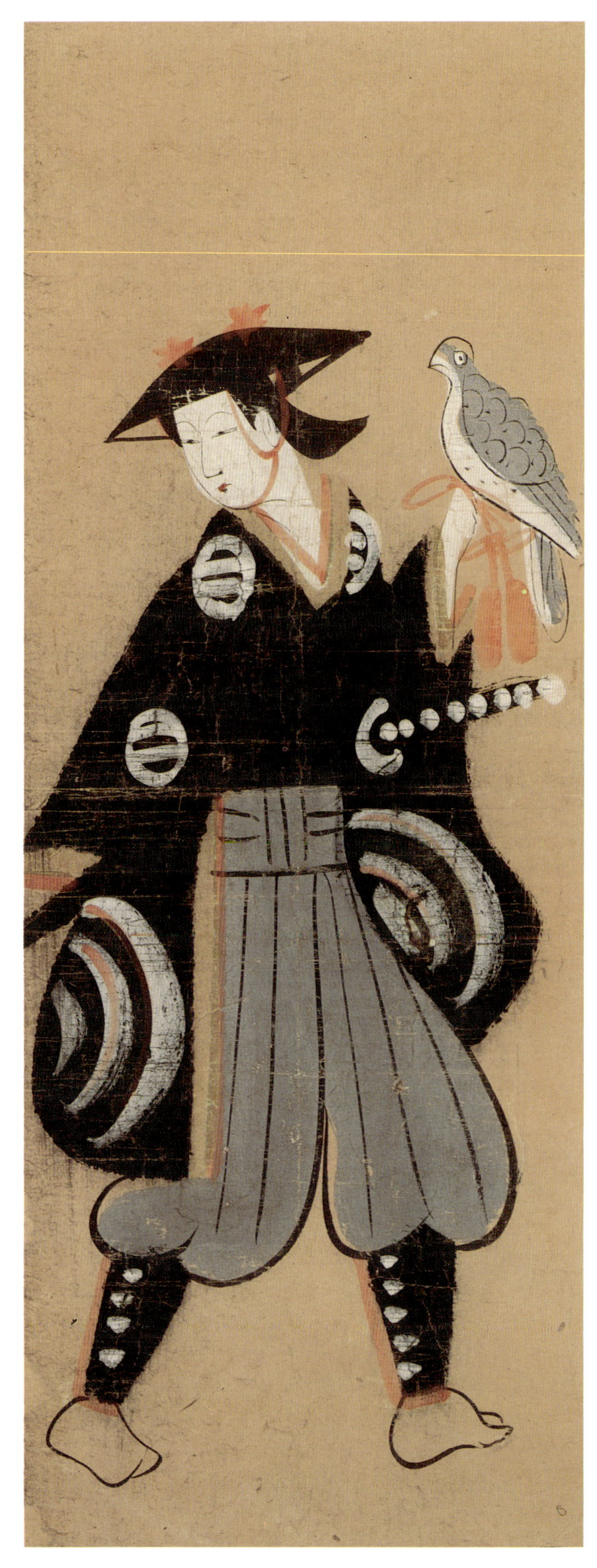

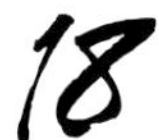

Falconer (*Takajō*)
18th century
Hanging scroll; ink and colors on paper
23⅛ × 8⅞ inches

Slightly later in date, this image of a falconer is better preserved than the previous example (cat. no. 17). The pigments are fresher, and the white patterns on the jacket, completely effaced on the earlier painting, are largely intact. Whereas the earlier falconer has the proud, masculine bearing of a young samurai, this one anticipates the look of later Ōtsu-e falconers—slightly built youths with delicate facial features, attired in increasingly flamboyant robes. They represented a fashion trend, prevalent during the eighteenth century, toward gorgeousness and extreme elegance, even among men. Stylistically, too, this impression is heightened by the thin, even brushwork outlining the figure and indicating the trouser pleats. Images of even later date exhibit the culmination of this trend: the falconer is attired in colorful robes with floral patterns on the dramatically long sleeves (fig. 3).

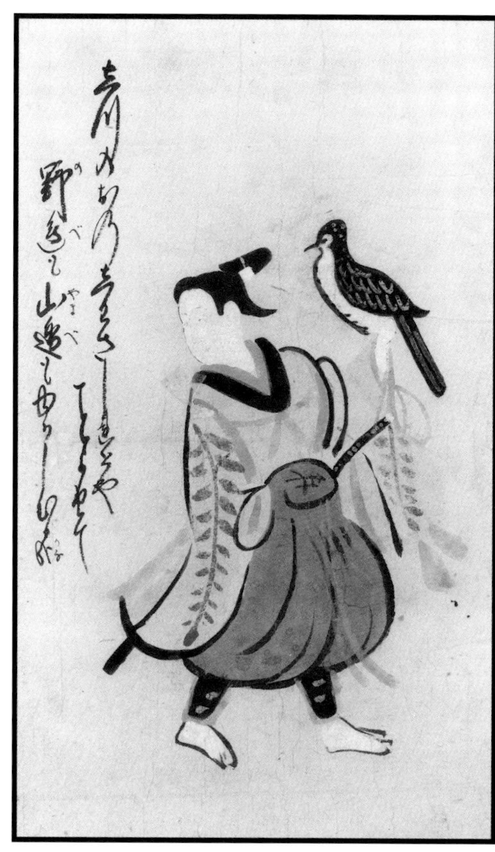

Fig. 3
Falconer
18th century
The Minneapolis Institute of Arts
Gift of Richard P. Gale

The popularity of the falconer theme may have had to do with a commonly held folk belief. To dream on New Year's about a falcon, eggplants, and Mount Fuji, it was said, portended a prosperous future. Many ukiyo-e artists cleverly juxtaposed all three of these elements in a single complex image. Although Ōtsu-e artists generally kept to the simple composition of a single figure, their falconer images were, nevertheless, probably purchased as lucky talismans. Indeed, in an interesting conflation of the pursuits of hunting and farming, people bought images of falconers in hopes of ensuring a good harvest.[1] The falconer remained a popular subject and was one of approximately ten themes that continued to be painted in great numbers during the twilight of Ōtsu-e production in the nineteenth century.

1. Kiyoshi Yokoi, *Early Ōtsu-e* (Tokyo: Mayuyama, 1958), p. 8.

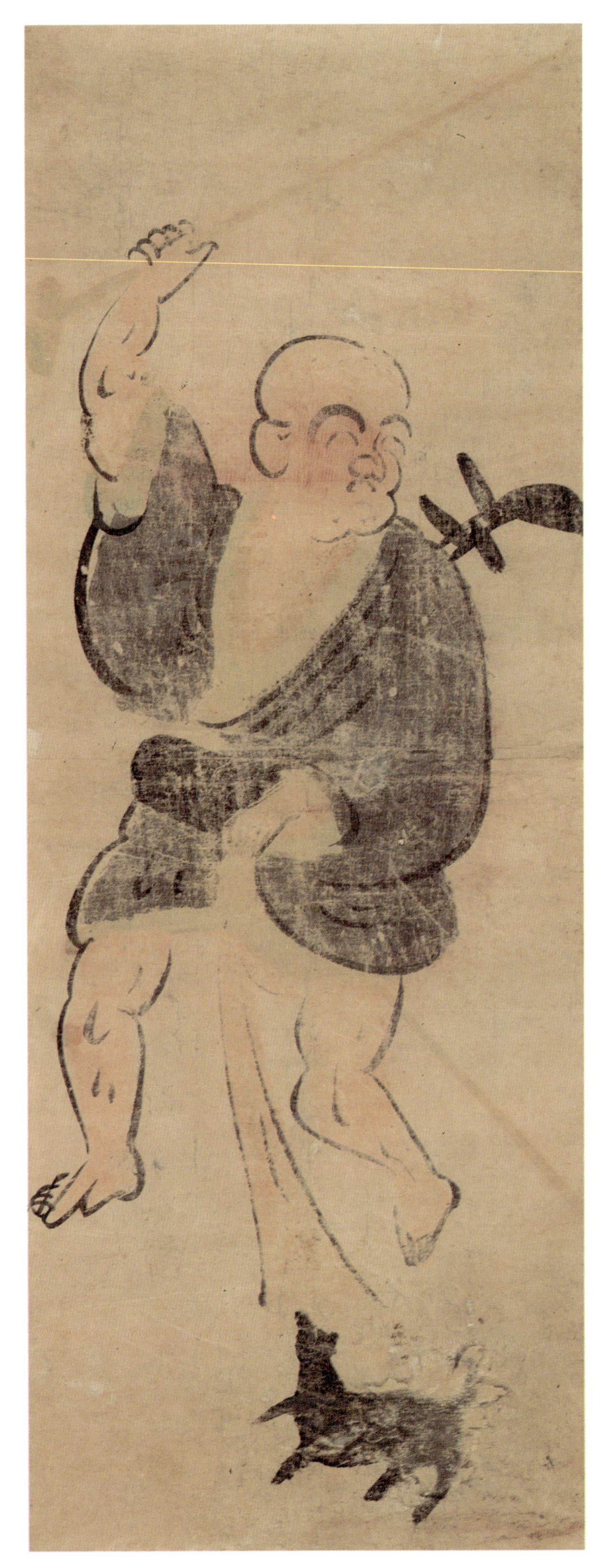

Blind Musician (*Zatō*)
18th century
Hanging scroll; ink and colors on paper
24¼ × 9³⁄₁₆ inches

As early as the seventh century, blind monks were trained to play the *biwa*, or lute, to accompany the chanting of Buddhist sutras. Later, during the Kamakura period (1185–1333), they retold the *Heike monogatari*, the epic story of the clashes between rival clans of the Taira and the Minamoto during the twelfth century. By the Edo period (1600–1868), the services offered by blind minstrels had expanded to include not only music and storytelling, but also massage and acupuncture. Catering to the needs of weary travelers, blind musicians made their living at roadside inns.

The minstrel in this Ōtsu-e has the shaved head and black robes of a Buddhist monk and carries a *biwa* strapped to his back. He is an unlucky man, for his loose loincloth has attracted the attention of an annoying little dog. Raising his cane high in the air, he tries to strike the tiny beast, but its frenetic movements and small size make it a difficult target. Meanwhile, more and more of his loincloth unravels.

Blind minstrels were a fairly common subject among artists of the Edo period. Rather than simply making light of them, however, the images usually function as allegories. The Zen priest Hakuin Ekaku (1685–1768), for example, painted blind men attempting to cross a log bridge, likening their cautious but deliberate progress to the tenacious spirit necessary to become "insightful," or enlightened. Other painters illustrated a group of blind men encountering an elephant. Each man examines, through touch, a different part of the creature's enormous body; and each forms a different notion of the elephant's nature, based on the part he experienced. Similarly, truth and reality, for the sighted as well as the blind, are partial and subjective.

While neither this painting nor catalogue number 20 bears an inscription, didactic poems added to later images suggest the Ōtsu-e artists' intent: "Be warned! If the lock of your mind gets loose, even a dog can take you by surprise."[1]

1. Kiyoshi Yokoi, *Early Ōtsu-e* (Tokyo: Mayuyama, 1958), p. 8.

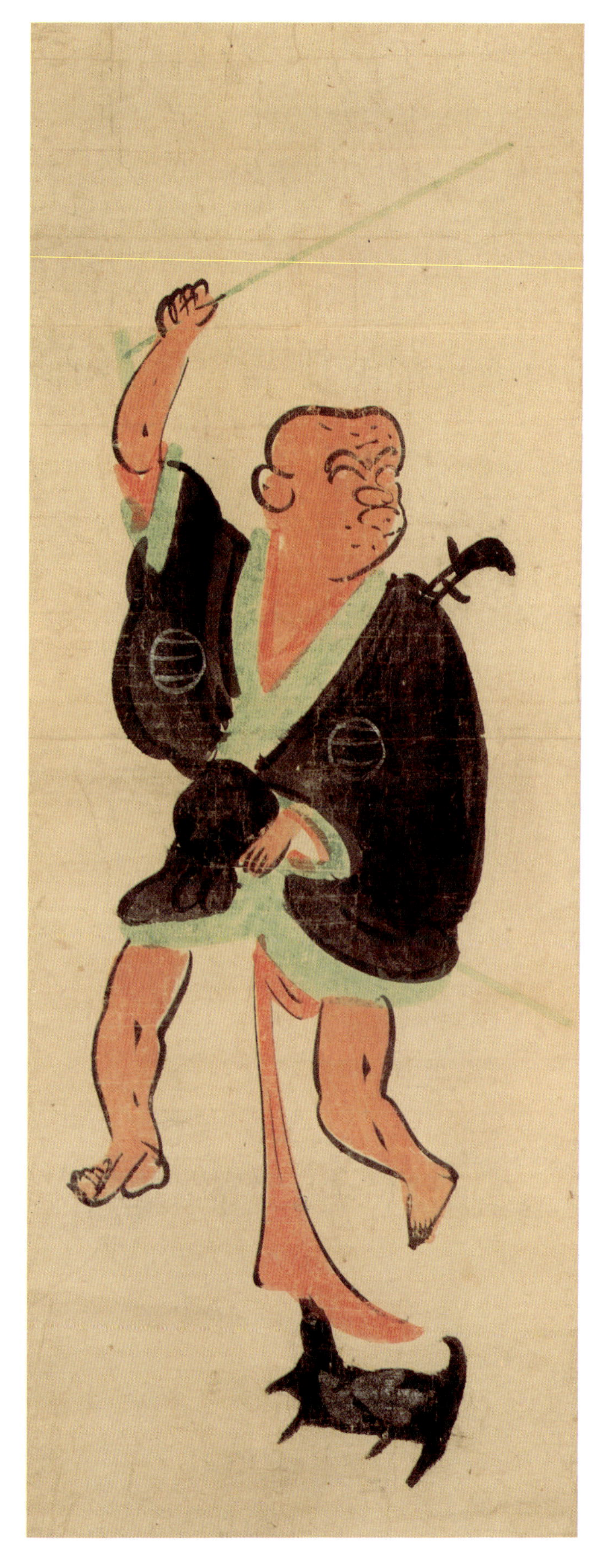

20

Blind Musician (*Zatō*)
Late 18th century or 19th century
Hanging scroll; ink and colors on paper
25⅜ × 9½ inches

Nearly identical in overall conception and pose to the previous work (cat. no. 19), this painting illustrates how Ōtsu-e subject matter was copied again and again, often without thought of artistic variation, in order to speed production. It is much more tentative and abbreviated than the other example, which displays considerable bravura in the ink brushwork outlining the figure. Here, the figure itself is slightly smaller and somehow less lively. Nevertheless, the freshness of the colors, owing to the later date, indicates the simple yet pleasing palette used by Ōtsu-e artists.

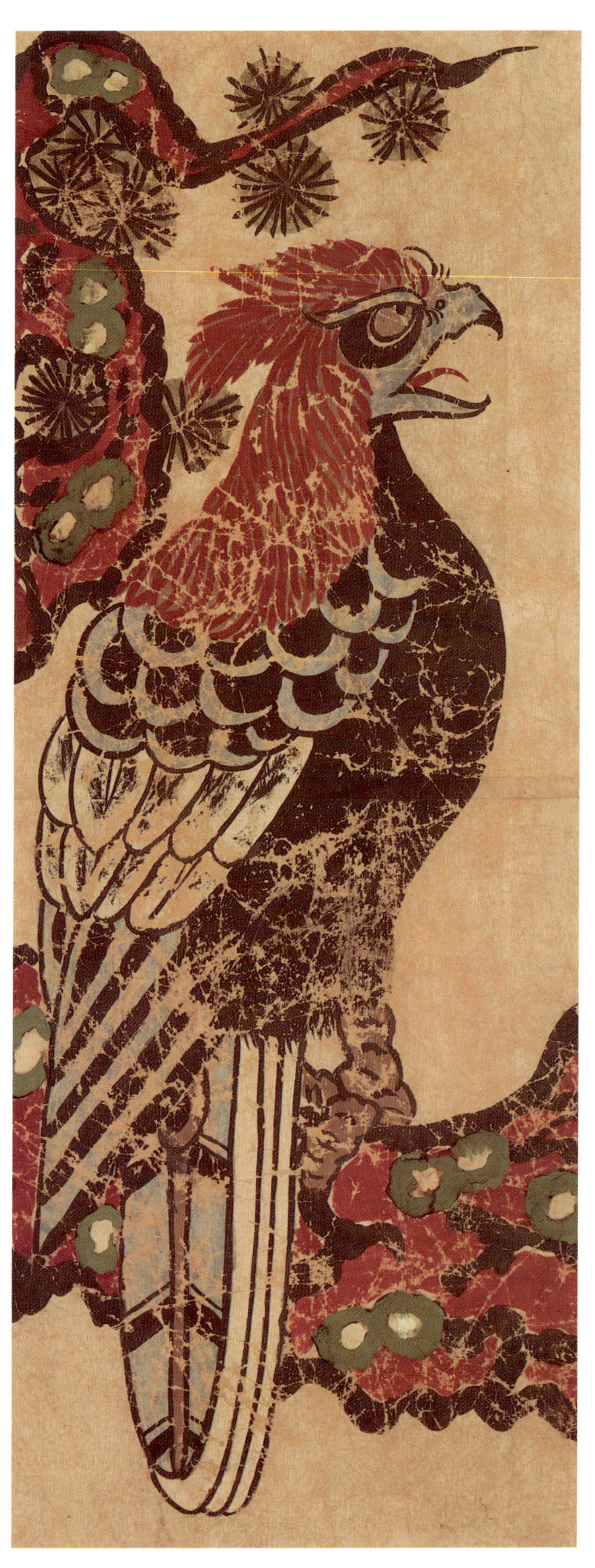

21

Eagle (*Washi*)
18th century
Ink and colors on paper
22½ × 9 inches

Japanese artists began to paint birds of prey during the Muromachi period (1333–1573), probably inspired by images imported from China. The subject appealed to the warrior class of Japan, for whom falconry had long been a favorite pastime. Under warrior patronage, artists produced numerous decorative folding screens and hanging scrolls showing these great birds in the act of capturing prey or poised, eyes gleaming, ready to strike. Like tigers, horses, and mythical beasts, birds of prey symbolized the physical strength and cunning of well-trained warriors.

During the Edo period (1600–1868), interest in birds of prey and falconry was not limited to aristocrats and warriors. Ukiyo-e woodblock prints of proud, fierce birds were purchased by common townspeople.[1]

Surviving Ōtsu-e include images of hawks, peregrine falcons, and eagles. This ferocious eagle is perhaps the most impressive of all. Firmly perched on a gnarled pine branch, the glaring bird opens its beak as if issuing a piercing shriek. The bold palette of Ōtsu-e artists is particularly effective here, with brilliant red used both for the tree bark and for the bird's beautiful crest. Unconcerned with realism, the artist conveyed the bird's strength by simplifying its feathers, boldly outlining each one so that it looks as impenetrable as armor.

This extremely rare image probably dates from the early eighteenth century. Later paintings, executed more quickly, in an abbreviated style, lack the strength and dignity of this fine example.

1. For examples, see Donald Jenkins, *Ukiyo-e Prints and Paintings: The Primitive Period, 1680–1745* (Chicago: Art Institute of Chicago, 1971), pls. 78–81; Howard Link, *Primitive Ukiyo-e: From the James A. Michener Collection in the Honolulu Academy of Arts* (Honolulu: University Press of Hawaii, 1980), p. 59; Cynthea Bogel et al., *Hiroshige Birds and Flowers* (New York: Braziller, 1988), nos. 23 and 69.

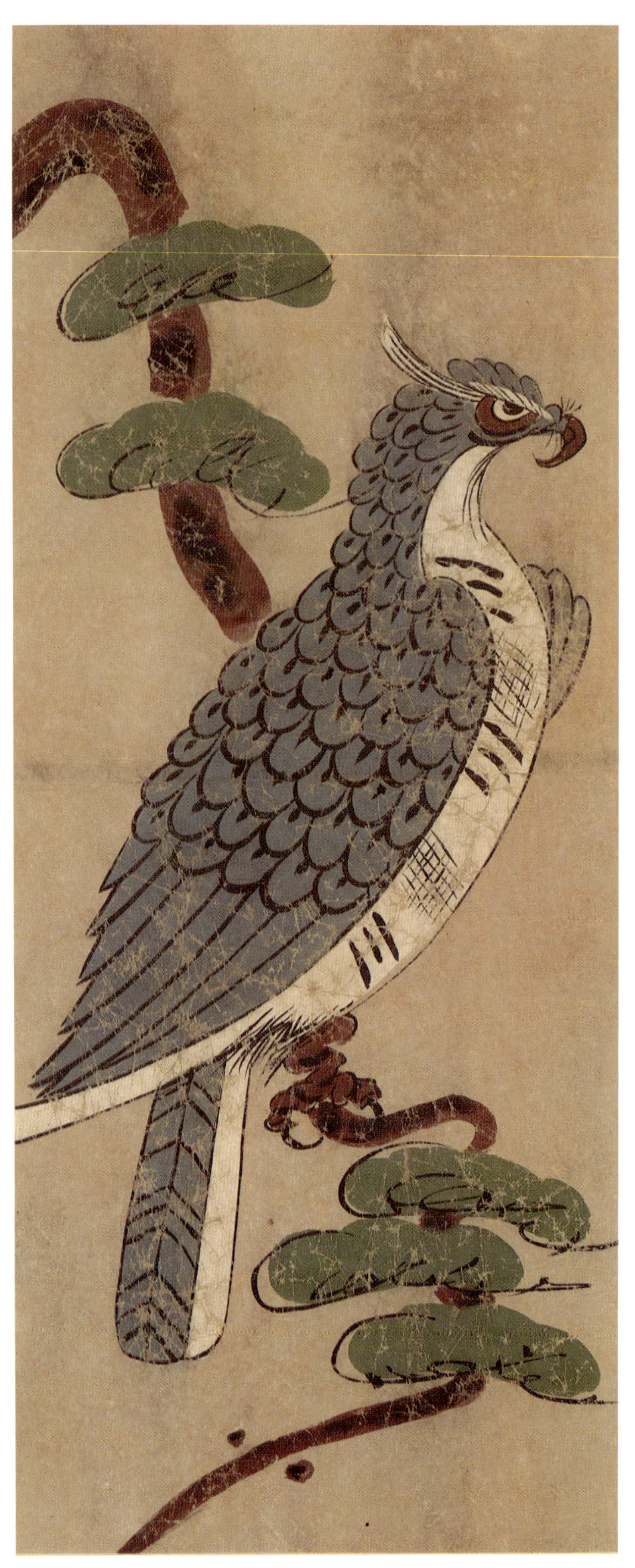

22

Peregrine Falcon (*Hayabusa*)
18th century
Ink and colors on paper
22¾ × 9¾ inches

Though falconry had been practiced in Japan from ancient times, interest in the sport seems to have increased during the Edo period (1600–1868). This may have been because Japan was at peace and samurai could devote themselves to cultivating such activities. In any case, birds of prey became standard subject matter for painters of every school.

The peregrine falcon, used for hunting small birds and animals, was prized for its speed. Here, swiftness is suggested by the streamlined profile, described with sweeping parallel strokes that deftly delineate the breast and wing. The bird's alert, tense posture is accentuated by the meandering pine branch, which seems hardly able to support its weight. The fierce eye and hooked beak leave no doubt as to the peregrine's deadly nature.

Perhaps because of the widespread fascination with these beautiful birds, the Japanese had a popular belief that good fortune awaited a person who dreamt about a falcon, an eggplant, and Mount Fuji on New Year's. Falcons were associated with focused endeavor leading to success, and eggplants symbolized fecundity. Fuji, revered as a sacred mountain, was unquestionably auspicious. Paintings of falcons may therefore have been purchased as much for their propitious meaning as for the beauty of the bird.

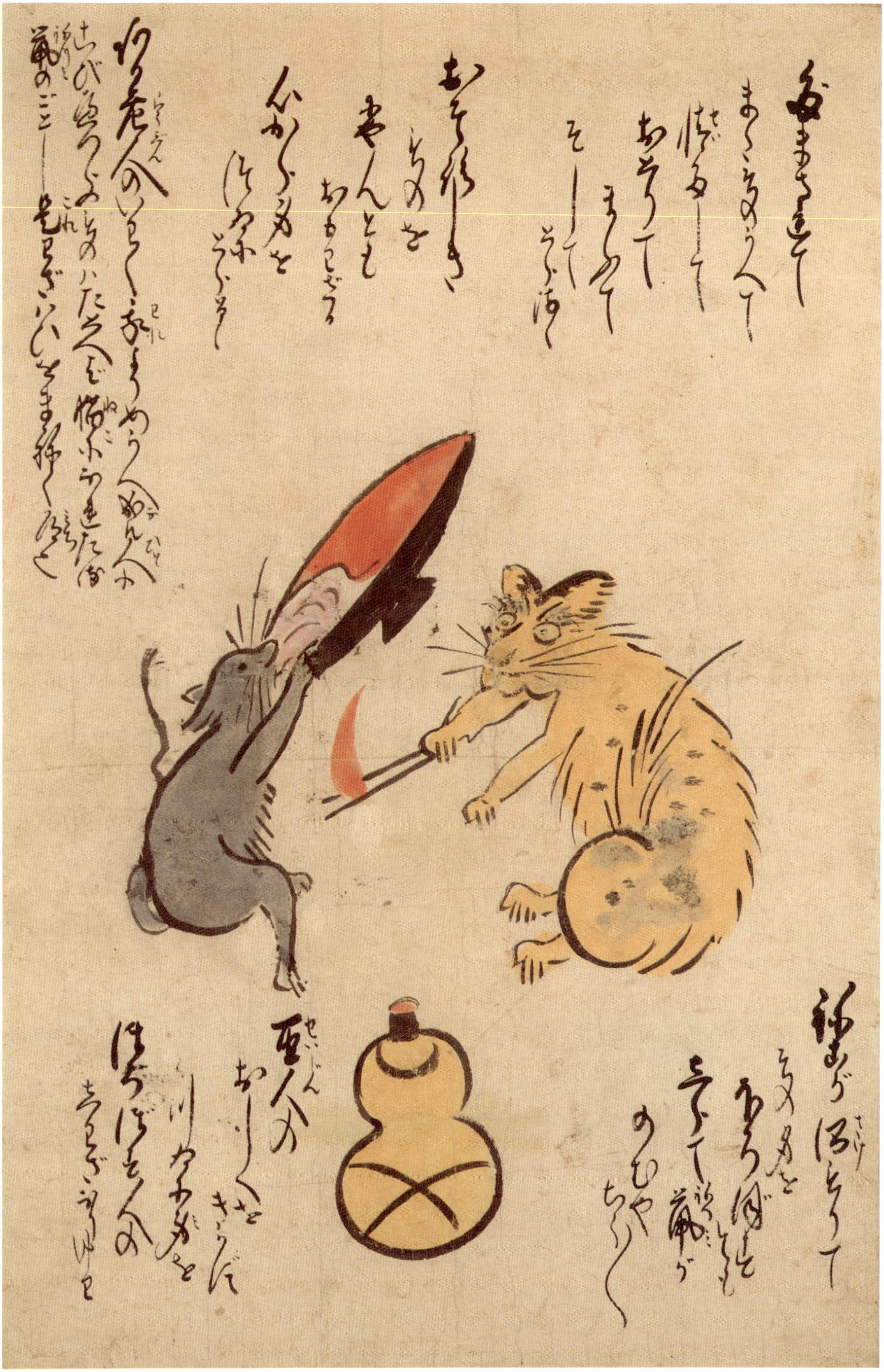

毎ままさ達て
まくろめうへて
悋(さ)がりして
おそうて
まして
そーして
そう済て

おそろしき
そのさ
やんとも
わかこぞう
ふかしぶみを
はなれ
そうぞし

此老人(らうじん)のいうことを(これ)まめうへめん(かひと)の
さらび[illegible]そのかたえ(これ)で猫(ねこ)から達た(かう)
鼠のごと[illegible]ゝ[illegible]と

酒(さけ)ありて
そのうへと
あらはしとも
そうて鼠が
のむや
ちゝし

聖人(せいじん)の
おしへを
きつけ
川[illegible]と

はらばらへの
[illegible]

23

Cat and Mouse (*Neko to nezumi*)
18th century
Hanging scroll; ink and colors on paper
16⅜ × 10 15/16 inches

Inscriptions:

Damasarete mata sono ue ni
Seidashite odorite moute
soshite toraruru
More than just deceived, [the mouse]
gleefully dances, and then is caught

Osoroshiki mono o nyan to
omowazaru kokoro kara mi o
tsui ni toraruru
The mind which does not heed danger
causes the body to be caught

Neko ga sake morite sono mi o
horobasu tomo shirate nezumi ga
nomu ya chiu chiu
Unwittingly befriended by the cat
who plies him with *sake*
the mouse drinks, slurp, slurp

Seijin no oshie o kikasu
tsui ni mi o horobosu hito no
shiwaza nari keri
Those who imitate the sages' teachings
will eventually ruin others' lives

Eyes wide in anticipation, the cat daintily offers a hot pepper with his chopsticks, knowing that it will make the foolish mouse gulp his *sake* more greedily. Oblivious of danger, the mouse tips the red and black lacquer cup to his lips. In the foreground stands a double gourd, used to decant the strong rice wine that is the cause of the mouse's reckless abandon and, ultimately, the cat's good fortune. The inscriptions reinforce the moralistic theme of the work: disaster awaits those who forget themselves and drink too much.

The Japanese have long delighted in the idea of animals parodying the actions of humans. Perhaps the most famous examples are the *Chōjū giga* handscrolls, painted during the twelfth century, which show monkeys, rabbits, and frogs engaging in various human activities such as wrestling, swimming, and even offering prayers before a solemn Buddha—in the shape of a frog.

Ōtsu-e artists, too, painted animals as a means of gently poking fun at human folly. A foolish monkey, for instance, is depicted trying to catch a catfish with a smooth gourd, a reference to a famous Zen koan (see cat. no. 24). In other Ōtsu-e an elephant and a *tengu* (a mythical mountain goblin) spar with their long noses, each jealous of the other's endowment.

Ōtsu-e artists began painting images of the cat and mouse in the early eighteenth century. The theme has several variations. In some paintings the situation is reversed, and the cat drains the cup, egged on by the mouse. Presumably the mouse intends to beat a hasty retreat when the cat is too drunk to give chase.

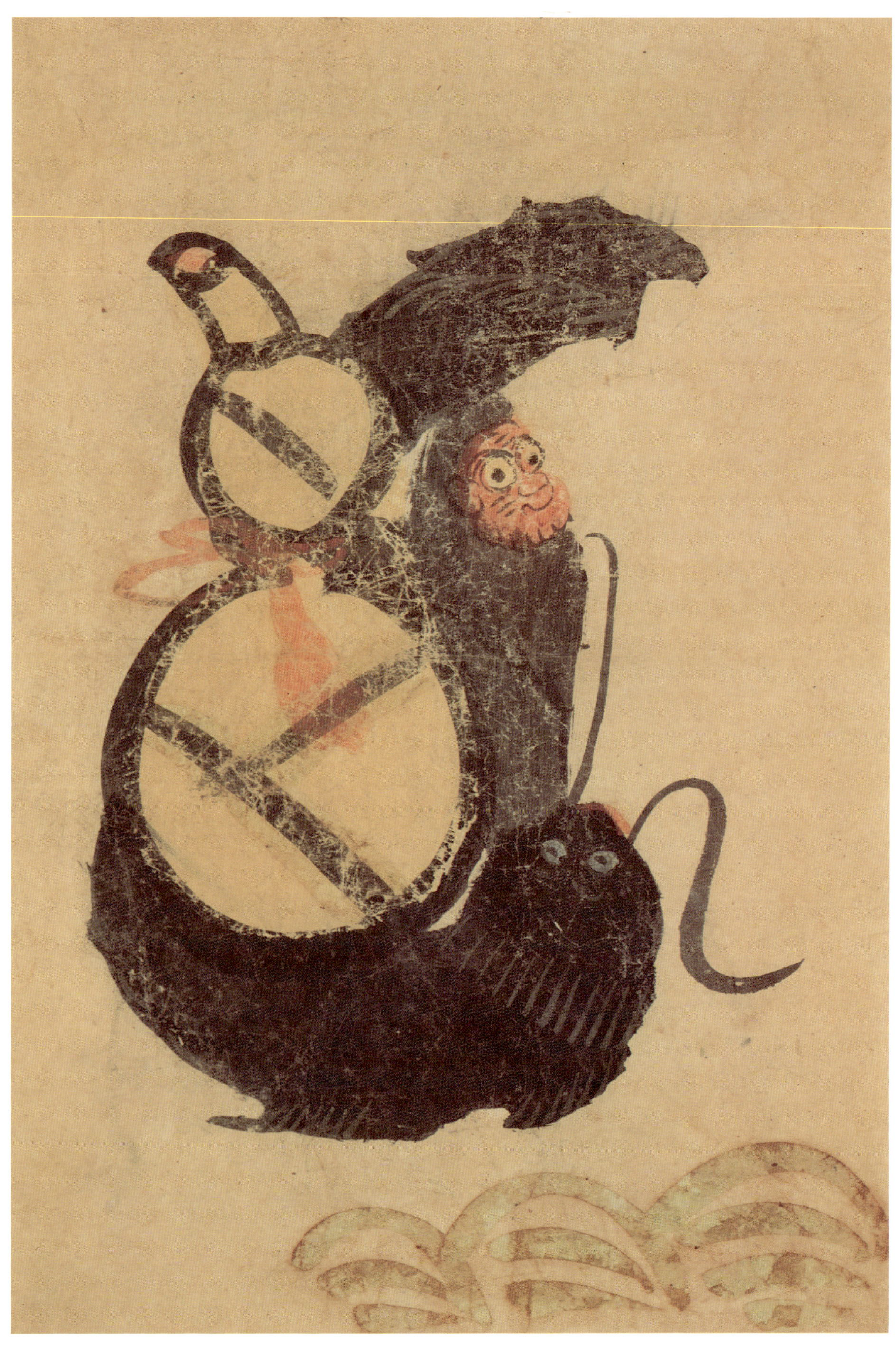

24

Catching a Catfish with a Gourd

(*Hyōtan namazu*)
18th century
Hanging scroll; ink and colors on paper
13 × 9 inches

"How to catch a slippery catfish with a smooth gourd" is a famous koan, a seemingly nonsensical question asked by a Zen master in hopes of prompting his pupils to go beyond the limitations of logical thought. Clearly, one is unlikely to trap the slippery fish by pressing it into the mud with a smooth gourd. Nor will any amount of patient coaxing entice the fish to swim into the tiny opening at the end of the gourd. The Ōtsu-e artist's conception is delightfully whimsical. A diminutive, red-faced monkey, dwarfed by his own gourd, is surrounded by the catfish, leaving one to wonder who has captured whom.

The subject was first painted by the monk Josetsu at the request of Shogun Yoshimochi in the early fifteenth century. Now in the collection of Myōshin-ji temple in Kyoto, Josetsu's painting shows a deluded country ruffian trying to capture a catfish in a stream by means of an ineffectual gourd. Metaphorically, the painting illustrates the futility of trying to "catch" truth by any other means than intuition.

Another interpretation of the catfish and gourd theme stems from an ancient legend, according to which the Japanese provinces of Hitachi and Shimōsa (present-day Ibaraki and Chiba) rested on the back of a giant catfish. When the fish moved, the land trembled with terrible earthquakes. The gods Takemikazuchi and Futsunushi were sent to make the area safe for Ninigi-no-mikoto, the grandson of the sun goddess, who was destined to descend to earth. Takemikazuchi drove his great sword into the earth, and as he did so, it turned into a column of stone, which pressed upon the back of the fish. Futsunushi, on the other hand, held the creature in place with his magic gourd.[1]

Ōtsu-e artists apparently took a pragmatic view of both traditions. By painting a monkey, an animal associated with foolish antics, they suggested the folly of trying to capture a fish with a gourd. Although this painting is not inscribed, a verse commonly found on other images reinforces the absurdity of the idea.

Michi naranu mono o hoshigari
yamasaruno kokoro kara to ya
uchi ni shizuman

A mountain monkey
wanting what it should not have
sank into the deep water

First painted by Ōtsu-e artists in the early eighteenth century, images of a monkey trying to catch a catfish remained popular throughout the succeeding century. Ironically, they were collected as talismans against drowning—in which case they were simply interpreted as a monkey clinging to a buoyant float. There exist a few early double-sheet compositions of a large catfish descending vertically, surmounted by the monkey and his gourd. The circular composition of this work, however, is particularly effective. The ragged outlines, caused by using stencils to block in large areas of color, contribute to the simple charm and informality of the subject.

1. T. Volker, *The Animal in Far Eastern Art* (Leiden: E. J. Brill, 1975), p. 124.

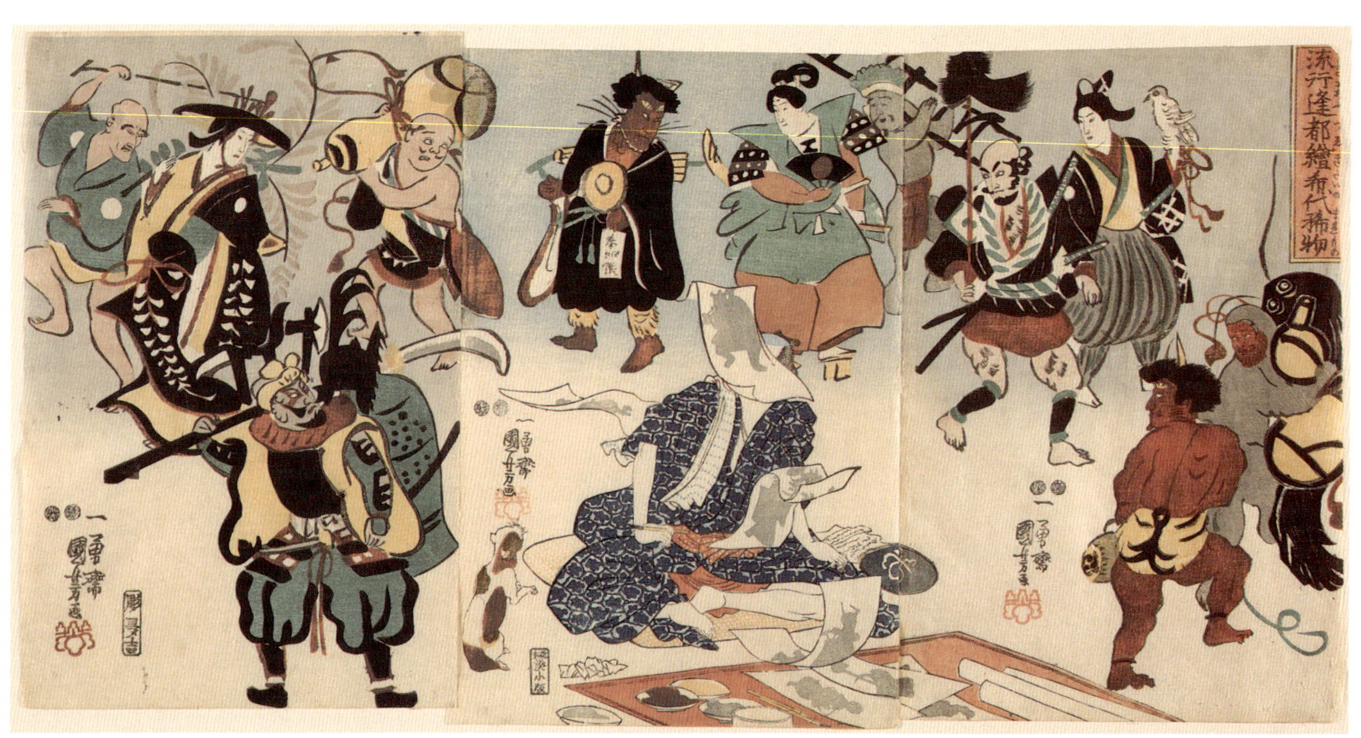
流行逢都繪希代稀物

25

Utagawa Kuniyoshi (1797–1861)
Rare Scrolls of Popular Ōtsu-e
(*Ryūkō Ōtsu-e kitai no makimono*)
About 1847–52
Color woodblock print
Ōban triptych, each print approximately
15 × 10 inches

Inspired by the public's interest in the lives of famous artists, the renowned playwright of the puppet theater (*jōruri*) Chikamatsu Monzaemon wrote a story whose main characters were loosely based on artists of the past. Entitled *Keisei hangonkō* (The Beauty Whose Spirit Appears in the Incense Smoke), it was first performed at the Takemoto theater in Osaka in 1708. One of the many subplots involves a certain Matahei (based on the artist Iwasa Matabei), who is credited with creating the Ōtsu-e style. In the story, Matahei is a poor artist with a speech impediment. With the help of his devoted wife, he ekes out a meager living by selling his paintings in Ōtsu and Oiwake. He aspires to be adopted into the artistic lineage of his teacher, the famous painter Tosa Shōgen (a conflation of Tosa Mitsunobu and Kanō Masanobu, whose art name was Shōgen). When Shōgen chooses another pupil, the dejected Matahei decides to kill himself, but first he paints a self-portrait on the side of a stone water-basin. The touch of his brush is so powerful that the image penetrates the stone and appears on the other side. Astonished at this feat, Shōgen changes his mind and accepts Matahei as his artistic heir.[1]

Over a hundred years later, the ukiyo-e artist Utagawa Kuniyoshi illustrated another of the play's dramatic episodes in two woodblock compositions (see also cat. no. 26). Matahei is about to be arrested on false charges, but the subjects of his paintings magically come to life and defend him. In both works, Matahei sits amid his painting materials and the Ōtsu-e characters dance around him, striking characteristic poses. Before transforming into the Ōtsu-e characters they represent, the paintings rise from the floor and flutter through the air.

Fascination with Ōtsu-e and the story of Matahei was not Kuniyoshi's only motive for producing these compositions. He was flouting a series of repressive government edicts that forbade the depiction of certain subjects deemed socially inappropriate or politically subversive. In this triptych he substituted the faces of well-known Kabuki actors for the Ōtsu-e characters' faces.[2] Benkei (in the lower half of the left print) even wears *kumadori*, the dramatic Kabuki makeup.

Kuniyoshi's mischief went beyond his "disguised" actor portraits. Matahei, his face obscured by a piece of airborne paper, is in fact a self-portrait of Kuniyoshi, identified by the paulownia crest on the round fan at his side and by the presence of his favorite cat.[3]

1. Samuel L. Leiter, *Kabuki Encyclopedia: An English-Language Adaptation of Kabuki Jiten* (Westport, Conn.: Greenwood Press, 1979), p. 188.
2. Sarah E. Thompson, "The Politics of Japanese Prints," in *Undercurrents in the Floating World: Censorship and Japanese Prints*, by Sarah E. Thompson and H. D. Harootunian (New York: Asia Society Galleries, 1991), pp. 65–68.
3. Ibid.

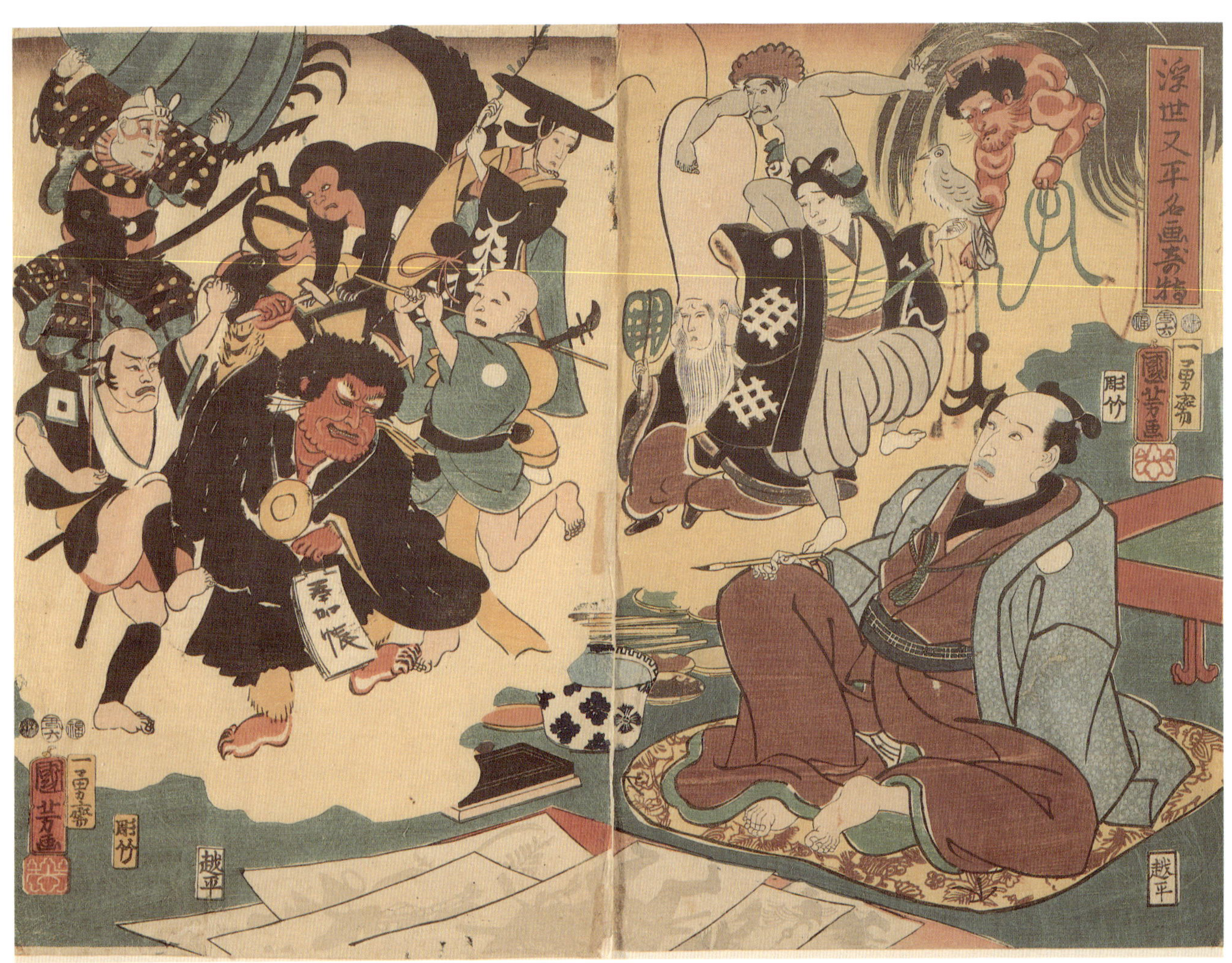
浮世又平名画奇特
一勇斎
國芳画
彫竹
越平
奉加帳
一勇斎
國芳画
彫竹
越平

26

Utagawa Kuniyoshi (1797–1861)
The Miracle of Famous Paintings by Ukiyo Matahei
(*Ukiyo Matahei meiga no kitoku*)
1853
Color woodblock print
Ōban diptych, each print approximately 15 × 10 inches

This diptych, like catalogue number 25, represents the dramatic scene in Chikamatsu's play *Keisei hangonkō* in which the artist Matahei's characters come to life to defend him from false arrest. Here, an astonished Matahei peers up at his creations. (His blue upper lip is meant to suggest his speech impediment.) Kuniyoshi incorporated all ten Ōtsu-e themes—the standard repertoire of Ōtsu-e artists after the turn of the nineteenth century.

In flouting government censorship, Kuniyoshi was even more daring here than in the triptych (cat. no. 25), brashly making light of the new shogun and his entourage by substituting their faces for those of the Ōtsu-e characters. For example, the falconer has the face of the shogun Iesada himself and the wisteria maiden that of his main consort Fujie. The spear bearer is the governor of Kishū (Wakayama), and the monkey riding the catfish is Torii Tadakiyo, both advisers to the shogun.[1] This violation did not go unnoticed, and the government censors levied fines against the disrespectful artist and his publisher.[2]

That Kuniyoshi chose the legend of Matahei as the vehicle for these "disguised" portraits suggests the degree to which Ōtsu-e had become part of Japanese culture by the nineteenth century. Kuniyoshi could assume not only that the public knew the story of Matahei as created by Chikamatsu, but also that they would recognize popular Ōtsu-e themes and delight in his reproduction of the Ōtsu-e style.

1. Ono Tadashige, "Ōtsu-e kō," in *Kaidō ni umareta minga: Ōtsu-e* (Kyoto: Korin-sha, 1991), p. 240.
2. Sarah E. Thompson, "The Politics of Japanese Prints," in *Undercurrents in the Floating World: Censorship and Japanese Prints*, by Sarah E. Thompson and H. D. Harootunian (New York: Asia Society Galleries, 1991), p. 65.

Bibliography

Art populaire japonais: 17e–19e siècle. Paris: Galerie Janette Ostier, 1962.

Hauge, Victor, and Takako Hauge. *Folk Traditions in Japanese Art.* New York: Weatherhill, 1978.

Kaidō ni umareta minga: Ōtsu-e. Kyoto: Korin-sha, 1991.

Katagiri Shozō. "Ōtsu-e no rekishi—minzoku toshite no Ōtsu-e." *Mingei* 397 (January 1986): 3–7.

Kobayashi Tadashi. *Ōtsu-e.* Machida: Machida Municipal Museum, 1990.

Kodansha Encyclopedia of Japan. 9 vols. Tokyo: Kodansha, 1983.

Mingei: The Living Tradition in Japanese Arts. Japan Folk Crafts Museum, Glasgow Museums, Kodansha International, 1991.

Munsterberg, Hugo. *Folk Arts of Japan.* Rutland, Vermont, and Tokyo: Tuttle, 1958.

Sansom, George. *A History of Japan, 1334–1615.* 1961. Reprint, Stanford, Calif.: Stanford University Press, 1987.

Yanagi Sōetsu. *Ōtsu-e zuroku.* Tokyo: Sansaisha, 1960.

———. "Ōtsu-e no hanashi." *Mingei* 354 (June 1982): 43–50.

———. "Introduction to Ōtsu-e." *Mingei* 397 (January 1986): 8–9.

———. "Ōtsu-e no bi to sono seihitsu." *Mingei* 430 (October 1988): 2–9.

———. "Daruma to Tenjin." *Mingei* 449 (May 1990): 7–8.

———. "Ōtsu-e no waka." *Mingei* 449 (May 1990): 2–6.

Yokoi, Kiyoshi. *Early Ōtsu-e.* Tokyo: Mayuyama, 1958.